THE NEW BRIDGES

THE CAUSEWAY TO ST IVES BRIDGE

by

Bridget Flanagan

ISBN 0-9540824-2-7

68 Common Lane
Hemingford Abbots
Huntingdon
Cambridgeshire PE28 9AW

Publication of this book has been made possible by a generous grant from the Goodliff Fund of the Huntingdonshire Local History Society.

Any profits from the sale of the book will go to The Friends of the Norris Museum.

Printed and Bound in Great Britain by Parrot Print Ltd. Ramsey, Cambs.
Pre-Press by Morgans Digital Repro. St Ives, Cambs.

The photograph across the front and back cover shows the New Bridges as seen from the Hemingford Meadow.

Acknowledgements

I followed up a suggestion made by Alan Wright at the end of his talk on the structural condition of the New Bridges to the Civic Society of St Ives: *it would be interesting to find something of the history of the New Bridges.* Little did I realise the amount of material to be discovered about the New Bridges, or that it would result in a book.

There are so many friends and helpers without whom this book would not have been achieved. I thank Bob Burn-Murdoch for drawing the maps, and for his endless good humour when I have interrupted him from his work over the last eighteen months. But more than that, with his knowledge of St Ives and the researcher's treasure trove that is the Norris Museum, he has guided and encouraged this book. Secondly, I am indebted to Bridget Smith for her wisdom and infectious enthusiasm. Also, but in no order of precedence, to: Beth Davis, Alan Wright, Chris Jakes, Peter Ibbett, Tony Minter, Mary Carter, Philip Crack, Tony Hudson, Louise Brown, Paul Yeandle, Peggy Seamark, David Viles, and Derek Clifton. Also to the staff at the County Record Offices at Huntingdon, Cambridge and Bedford, the St Ives, Huntingdon, Cambridge and Newark Libraries, the Cambridgeshire Collection, the Institute of Civil Engineers, Cambridgeshire and Nottinghamshire County Council departments of Bridge Engineers, the House of Lords Record Office, the Public Record Office at Kew, English Heritage and the National Sites and Monuments Record, and The Georgian Society.

Old photographs and maps are reproduced with the kind permission of the County Record Office at Huntingdon, and the Norris Museum.

I am honoured that the Civic Society of St Ives has lent its support to this research about one of the major landmarks connected with the town.

Bridget Flanagan

Fig. 1 The New Bridges
The downstream side of the arches as viewed from Wilhorn Meadow looking towards St Ives.
Photo courtesy of The Cambridge Evening News

Introduction

The New Bridges are the southern causeway to St Ives Bridge and were built in 1822, replacing a series of old bridges.

To date, virtually nothing has been known about the New Bridges. But now the history of the New Bridges is uncovered. Some of the brief 'facts' previously attributed to the New Bridges are found to be incorrect and very misleading; in the light of fresh information the New Bridges emerge as an important and worthy part of St Ives' history. They deserve appreciation, and it is long over-due.

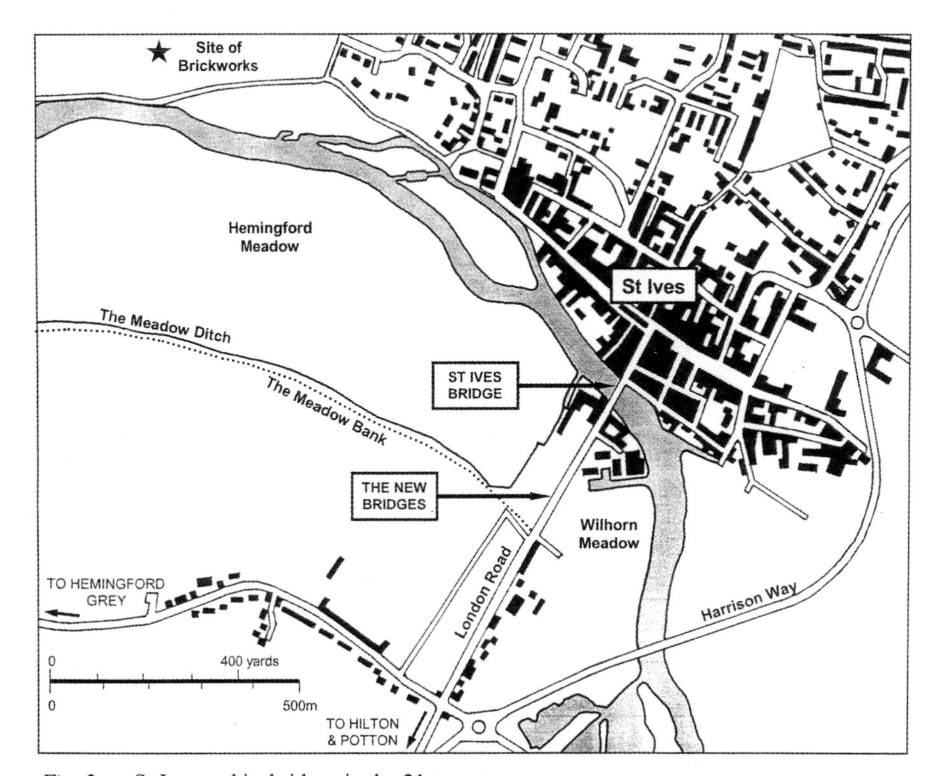

Fig. 2 St Ives and its bridges in the 21st century

Crossing the River Great Ouse at St Ives

There has been a crossing point on the River Great Ouse at St Ives for at least a thousand years; in "St Ives Bridge and Chapel" Bob Burn-Murdoch explains the evidence for a ford dating from Saxon times. But this route across the river was probably established much earlier. It may have been used by the Roman settlement at St Ives, and before that by the various peoples who have left scattered archaeological remains testifying to their existence in this part of the Great Ouse valley.

However a bridge is a preferred method of river crossing to a ford (or ferry) and consequently, where circumstances allow, a bridge replaces a ford. At St Ives, the physical characteristics necessary for the site of the original ford were also particularly suitable for the building of a bridge; the gravel bed of the river allowed for good foundations for the bridge, and the shallow waters aided its construction.

The Great Bridge of St Ives

The first known reference to a bridge at St Ives is in a document of 1107:

> *the meadow on which the bridge is built, as much of it as lies between the bridge and the end of the ford.*

These details describe part of the site of St Ives Bridge: the northern end of the bridge is within the town of St Ives sited on the gravel terraces above flood level, whereas the southern end of the bridge is in a meadow on the river's wide, low-lying flood plain. 'Flood meadows' are, as their name explains, frequently flooded by the river, and, because the water table is close to the surface, their ground can be soft for many months of the year. In their natural form flood meadows have an outer ditch or stream at the point where the ground level rises above the flood plain of the river. The 1107 reference to St Ives Bridge mentions a secondary crossing of water – *the ford* - and it can be presumed that this ford crossed the ditch which was then part of what is known today as the Hemingford Meadow Drain.

St Ives Bridge, the meadow and a small bridge are described 150 years later in the testimony to an inquest in 1259. Richard, son of Lucy from Bury St Edmunds, fell off St Ives Bridge and was drowned:

> *the body of the deceased was found on the land to the south of the great bridge of St Ives between the bridge itself and a certain small bridge.*

This *small bridge* is the earliest description of a part of the causeway.

The word 'causeway' was generally used in medieval times as 'causey' or 'causeyway'. It means a raised path, often along the top of an embankment, across low, wet ground. The derivations are various but linked, and amongst others are: 'calcare' – to stamp down, 'calceare' – to shoe, and 'chaussee' – paved. Hence a bank made of stamped earth, and a dry and a paved way. The term 'causeway' also has connections with the 'highway' of the Romans - a raised, stone-built road.

And so it can be deduced that, at St Ives, the causeway comprised small bridges over the natural watercourses within the meadow, and, for the rest of its length in between the bridges, there was a raised earth embankment which may have had a covering of stones or brushwood.

A Causeway to St Ives Bridge

By the 13th century St Ives had developed significantly under the rule of the commercially astute Benedictine Abbey at Ramsey. The cult of St Ivo brought pilgrims to the growing town whilst the Fair brought merchants from all over England and parts of Europe. St Ives was the highest navigable point on the River Great Ouse after Ramsey Abbey and the de Grey family had built watermills which dammed the river at Houghton and Hemingford Grey. Whilst this caused an economic decline up-river at Huntingdon it had fortuitous advantages for St Ives' position as a distribution point for inland river-borne trade.

Travellers came to St Ives by river and road, and the town was perfectly placed to receive them; the provision of a bridge enhanced the established route across the river, and also allowed for development of the network of subsidiary roads that radiated from the river crossing. But the southern route across the meadow was a weak and wet link in the network. Clearly, a causeway was needed to cross the potentially difficult terrain of the flood plain, and to allow travellers safe, dry, year-round access to St Ives Bridge. A causeway is an integral part of a river crossing, and therefore it is probable that the building of a causeway soon followed the building of the river bridge, but there was one problem - the causeway and the bridge at St Ives were under separate ownership.

Pepper, Ginger and Eels

The Victoria County History of Huntingdonshire summarises various references to the causeway from ancient deeds, and records of Ramsey Abbey and the Crown. The first is dated 1238 and contains the necessary details of the commercial arrangements which were drawn up between the owner of the causeway - Hemingford Grey Manor, and the owner of St Ives Bridge - the Abbot of Ramsey:

> *The abbots of Ramsey paid yearly for its [the causeway's] use a pair of scarlet hose, 2lb of pepper, 2lb of ginger, 1000 eels, and allowed common rights in the abbey wood. In 1238 Alice, widow of Ralph Turbeville, [and as such, Lady of the Manor of Hemingford Grey] agreed to alter this rent to 40 cartloads of underwood from the wood of St Ives, 1000 eels and half a mark and further repayment for her life of 20 cartloads of wood.*

Alice Turbeville obviously understood the strategic and financial importance of the causeway and made sure that she received due recompense (and warmth) from the Abbot. Tough maintenance and rental negotiations continued:

> *The rent was again changed by John de Grey and his son Reginald in 1249-50 to 2 marks, and John and Reginald gave an undertaking to maintain the causeway.*

A later agreement was strongly drawn in favour of the causeway owner when it allowed him to exact financial penalties from the Abbot of Ramsey if St Ives Bridge was impassable:

> *The southern extension or causeway which passed over the land of the manor of Hemingford Grey as far as 'St Elyn's Cross' was rented from the lord of that manor, who amerced [fined] the abbot when the bridge was out of repair.*

During the dissolution of the monasteries in 1539, Henry VIII seized all the property of Ramsey Abbey and this included St Ives manor and the Bridge. The manor then changed hands several times until it was reacquired by the Crown in 1625. At some, but unknown, point one of the owners of St Ives manor bought the causeway from Hemingford Grey manor, for when Henry, Earl of Manchester, purchased St Ives manor in 1628 both the Bridge and the causeway became his property.

The Earls of Manchester (later to become Dukes) were granted a charter to levy tolls on the Bridge, and this charter contained an agreement for the maintenance of the causeway:

> *The Inhabitants of Fenstanton, Hemingford Grey, and Hemingford Abbotts are exempt from the above Passage Tolls provided that they cart Gravel when directed upon the Bridges and Roads for Repairs.*

After 400 years of complicated agreements between Bridge and causeway owners, the new single ownership promised simplicity. There would be greater control, freedom from rental arrangements, and in addition, the security of a constant toll income because St Ives Bridge would not be out of use due to the causeway being impassable.

Fig. 3 St Ives Bridge

The Road to St Ives Bridge

A comprehensive system of road and bridge maintenance in England came to an end with the dissolution of the monasteries. Until then the Church had largely organised the repair of national and local roads in order to facilitate its communications, commerce and pilgrims; the Church's manorial estates supplied the labour, and alms and penances from travellers provided the finance.

A new national administrative system was urgently needed, and some years later in 1555 a statute made parishes responsible for repairing their own roads. By 1563 parishioners had to spend six days a year working on the roads – their 'statute duty'. The Justices of the Peace could indict or prosecute a parish if its roads were not maintained, and then fines could be levied at the Quarter Sessions. Theoretically such a system should have provided well-maintained roads, but practically it was not effective, particularly where a parish had a main road going through it. Roads deteriorated throughout the country to the extent that they prevented any expansion of traffic.

The Turnpike road system which began in the 17th century and rapidly gathered pace in the 18th century was a commercial response to the urgent requirement for good roads. Acts of Parliament gave individual Trusts the power to borrow money for road works, and the power to collect tolls to repay those costs. (The word 'turnpike' originally referred to the long pole or pike placed across the road. This pivoted on a central point, and hence the 'turnpike' was where the traveller paid a toll for the pike to be turned allowing him to use the stretch of road ahead. Generally, a conventional gate or bar came to be used, but the name of turnpike stuck.)

The parishes' share of responsibility for road repair continued alongside the Turnpike Trusts until the early 19th century; the Trusts could either demand these repair works from a parish, or agree to commute the work through financial payments. The main national routes from London were among the first to be turnpiked because they were the most heavily used and generally, the most commercially important roads. Local, provincial roads followed and linked with existing turnpikes, and from 1750 a countrywide network of good roads began to emerge.

The Bury to Stratton Turnpike Trust

The Bury to Stratton Turnpike Trust was founded in 1755 to manage about 30 miles of road in Huntingdonshire, Cambridgeshire and Bedfordshire:

> *An Act for repairing the Road from a certain Place in Bury, in the County of Huntingdon, through Warboys, Old Hurst, Saint Ives, Hilton, Eltisley, Waresley, Gamlingay, and Potton, to a House called The Spread Eagle in the Hamlet of Stratton.*

Sadly very few of the Trust's documents have been kept. There are no Minute Books and no correspondence. All that remains is a 1754 road map and an Accounts Ledger covering the years 1826-54, both in the Huntingdon Record Office, and the Acts of Parliament which are in the House of Lords Record Office.

Fig. 4 The old causeway - (north is to the left)
The three small bridges can be seen on the left of the map, below Philip Miller's land; Helford Bridge adjoins William Barnes' land. This map, from the Manchester archives, is probably late 18th century; it pre-dates the 1801 Hemingford Grey Enclosure – note "Hemmingford Common Fields".
County Record Office, Huntingdon *SM16/107*

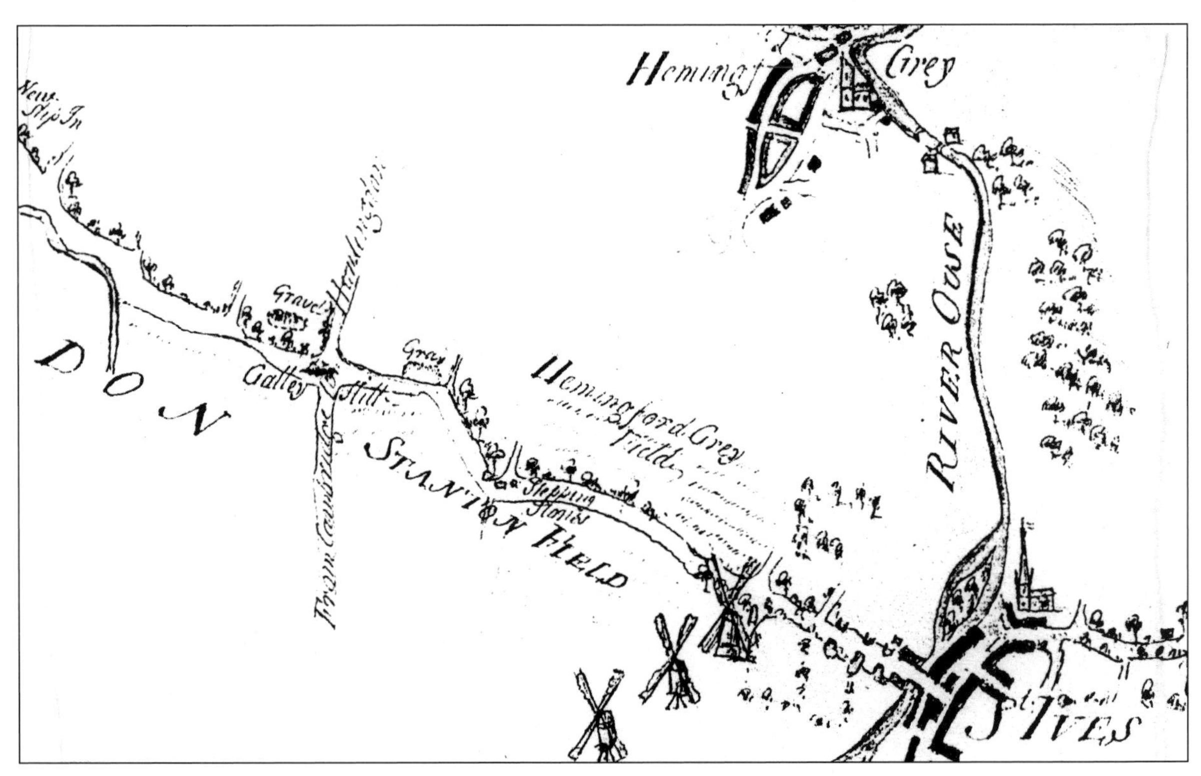

Fig. 5 Part of a map of the Bury-Stratton road, surveyed and drawn in 1754 by William Elstobb
This detailed map was not intended to be used by road travellers. Instead it was a survey of the road for the Turnpike Trust. This section shows sites where gravel for road repairs could be found. Features of the road include the major water-course of Hall Green Brook running beside the Hilton road, the Stepping Stones in the road in Hemingford Grey, St Ives Bridge and the old causeway bridges. Notable landmarks are the post mills along what is now the Fenstanton Low Road, the locks in the river at Hemingford Grey and Houghton, and the parish churches.
County Record Office, Huntingdon Acc 1590

The turnpiked road started at Bury, near Ramsey, travelled south through St Ives, crossed the River Great Ouse on St Ives Bridge, continued south to cross the Huntingdon–Cambridge road, then on to cross the Huntingdon–London road (Ermine Street), and ended at Stratton, near Biggleswade, at a junction with the Great North Road. Apart from providing important cross-country links, it was primarily a direct route towards London for the market town of St Ives in Huntingdonshire and, to a lesser extent, Potton in Bedfordshire. St Ives, with its Bridge, was pivotal to the Bury-Stratton road but, equally, the turnpiked road was vital to St Ives. The improved road gave St Ives better communications with its hinterland, and this facilitated and increased commerce in the town. As business grew so did the number of road users who generated an increase in toll income which paid for the road works; clearly, the initiative for road improvement came primarily from local commercial interests.

Most of St Ives' commerce was based on, or related to, its livestock markets for which the town was well situated, it being within suitable travelling distance of London. 18th century London, described by Daniel Defoe in 1722 as the *great center of England,* had a large, rapidly expanding population with an ever rising demand for provisions.

Drovers brought cattle to St Ives from Scotland, Ireland and the north of England. Some animals were marketed immediately, but those that came the greater distances were contracted to graziers to be fattened up on pastures around Huntingdonshire before being brought into St Ives market. Much of this 'meat on the hoof' was then sold on to London's Smithfield market; the cattle were taken south, wherever possible along 'green' or 'drove roads' to avoid towns, traffic and especially the paying of turnpike tolls. However Defoe noted the roads to the south of Huntingdonshire:

being worn by the drifts of cattle which come this way out of the fens of the Isle of Ely so constantly coming up to London markets.

Defoe also gave a first-hand account of the London-bound trade in ducks and geese from St Ives: *three thousand couple a week of wildfowl.* If the wagons of wildfowl were similar to those from Peterborough which *were drawn by ten and twelve horses a piece, they were loaden so heavy*, they would have caused deep ruts on unmade roads.

A road worn ruinous

In July 1810 a crisis began to unfold. The road to St Ives Bridge was in disrepair, and was described to the Quarter Sessions as:

the said part of the common King's Highway in the parish [is] so worn foul miry deep ruinous, broken washed away, lowered, overflowed and drowned and in such decay for want of due reparation and amendment....

The Duke of Manchester's estate had been paying for some (but obviously not sufficient) repairs to the old causeway; at this time the causeway comprised two single-arched wooden bridges, a larger wooden bridge called 'Great Helford Bridge' and a brick tunnel. Between 1805 and 1807, in the journal of George Skeeles, the St Ives builder, there are notes of bills to the Duke's surveyor for *work at bridges and repairing Helford Bridge.* On July 6th 1805 costs of labour and *planks, nails and oak* amounted to £10 – 6s- 4d.

But the Duchy was seemingly tired of this continual expenditure, and His Grace's agent, Mr Welstead explored how the costs might be defrayed. (William Montagu was the Fifth Duke of Manchester, having inherited the title when only 17 years old on the death of his father in 1788. The Fifth Duke spent very little time at the family seat at Kimbolton Castle; he was Governor of Jamaica from 1808 – 1827, Postmaster General from 1827 – 1830, and also Collector of Customs for the Port of London. He died in Rome in 1843. It is not certain how closely the Duke involved himself in the supervision of his Huntingdonshire estates.)

Mr Welstead requested the charge sheet for the Bridge tolls in order to see whether the rate of tolls on the Bridge could be raised to pay for the causeway repairs. It took some time for Mr Joseph Harris, a St Ives solicitor, to find this document but on July 5th 1810 he replied:

> *My List I had mislaid and could not lay my hand upon it till this morning – I think you have a right to advance [increase] the Tolls unless the same were fixed by the Grant or Charter which I have never seen.*

Mr Welstead read through the list and pencilled a 100% increase alongside most of the toll charges, e.g. *Bullocks, passage per score* he marked up from 4d to 8d. When he got to the end of the document he noticed Hemingford Grey's exemptions from the Tolls *provided that they cart Gravel for Repairs when directed.* He acted immediately. Within days, an Indictment on behalf of the Duke of Manchester was brought to the Quarter Sessions, which tried to force Hemingford Grey Parish to carry out road maintenance works. In their defence, two parishioners of Hemingford Grey - Poulter Margetts and William Fordham, gave a sworn statement; they robustly argued that the responsibility for road maintenance lay not with them, but with the owner of the ancient causeway – the Lord of the Manor of St Ives, the Duke of Manchester. They confirmed that:

> *the Lord of St Ives Manor, as such and by reasons of his tenure, of right ought to repair and amend the same when and as often as occasion or need hath required or shall require the same.*

Whilst these parties argued over the responsibility for the repairs, it seems that travellers continued to struggle through dreadful conditions along the inadequate old causeway.

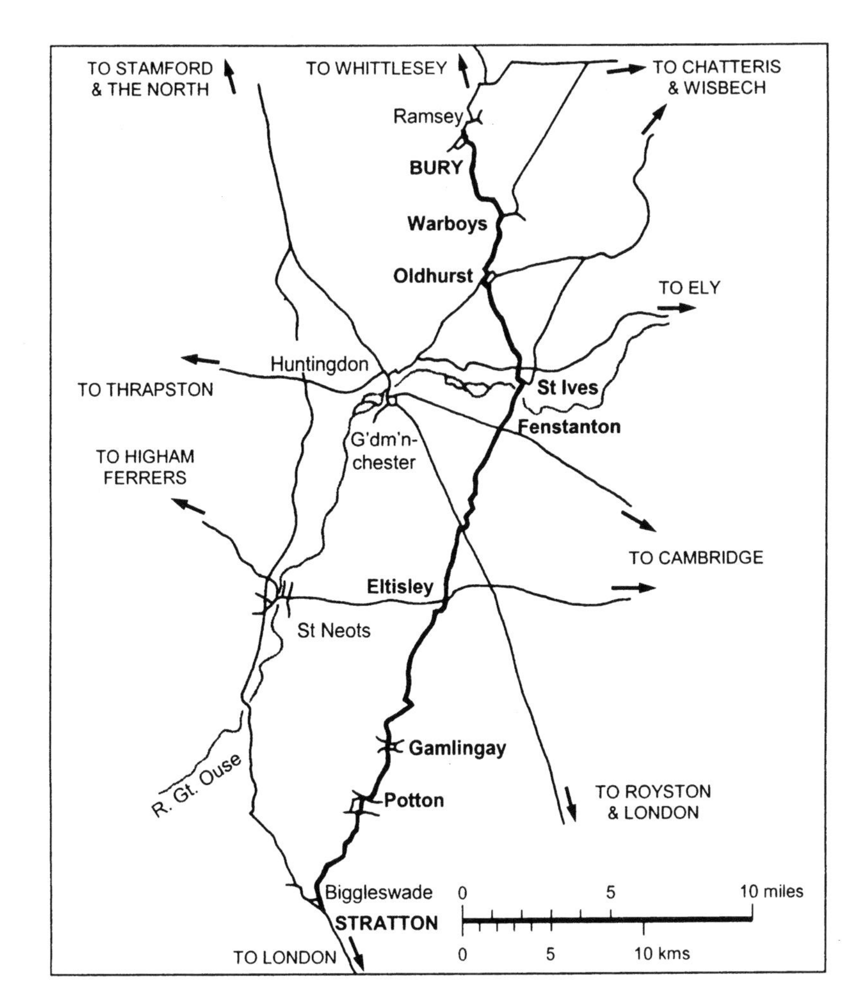

Fig. 6 The road from Bury to Stratton, turnpiked in 1755

Part of this road disappeared in the 20th century; Wyton Airfield was built across the Old Ramsey Road between St Ives and Oldhurst.

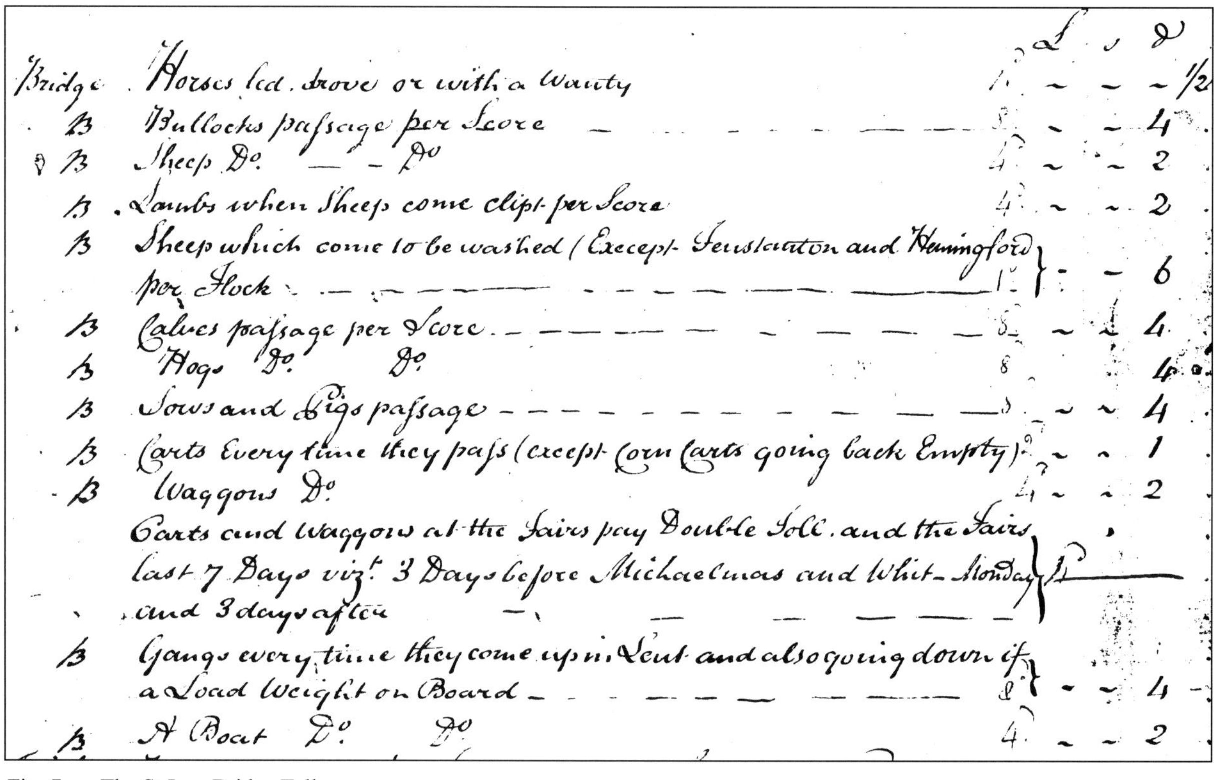

			£	s	d
Bridge	Horses led, drove or with a Wanty	1	–	–	½
B	Bullocks passage per Score	8	–	–	4
B	Sheep Do. — Do	4	–	–	2
B	Lambs when Sheep come clipt per Score	4	–	–	2
B	Sheep which come to be washed (Except Fenstanton and Hemingford) per Flock	1	–	–	6
B	Calves passage per Score	8	–	–	4
B	Hogs Do. Do.	8			4
B	Sows and Pigs passage	[illegible]	–	–	4
B	Carts Every time they pass (except Corn Carts going back Empty)	2	–	–	1
B	Waggons Do.	4	–	–	2
	Carts and Waggons at the Fairs pay Double Toll. and the Fairs last 7 Days viz.t 3 Days before Michaelmas and Whit-Monday and 3 days after				
B	Gangs every time they come up in Lent and also going down if a Load Weight on Board	8	–	–	4
B	A Boat Do. Do	4	–	–	2

Fig. 7 The St Ives Bridge Tolls

The faint numbers just to the left of the prices show where Mr Welstead, the Duke of Manchester's Agent, pencilled in suggestions of 100% increases. The tolls were fixed by a Royal Charter, granted in 1628. If the Duke had wished to raise the prices in 1810 he would have needed to seek Royal Assent.

Norris Museum, St Ives *UMS/KIMBN/139*

Plans for Improvement

Eight years later, in 1818, plans for improving the road were revealed by the Bury–Stratton Turnpike Trust. A Turnpike Trust's legal authority granted through an Act of Parliament had a term of only 21 years, after which a new Act was necessary. There had been renewal for the Bury-Stratton Trust in 1776 and 1797, and renewal was again necessary in 1818. A new Act was expensive, costing over £400, and so the Trust took the opportunity to combine an application for power to effect major repairs on the road with the necessary renewal, and placed notice of their intentions in the local newspapers

The new Act did not take effect until the first Tuesday in June 1819. The Trustees, all 178 of them, were individually named in the Act. Each was required to have either annual land or rental incomes of £100, or an estate of £3000, or be direct heirs to the same. These qualifications were a reflection of the 18th century and early 19th century assumption that the ownership of property, particularly land, carried with it the qualification, if not the positive right and responsibility to govern. All the Trustees were male and there were many family groups. The local aristocracy, Members of Parliament and land owners were well represented; these members of the ruling (and voting) class of society would have considered it their duty to be Trustees. There were a number of lawyers and JPs who were needed to give authority and legality for both the acquiring of the Act of Parliament and the administration of a Trust. The remaining group were businessmen and merchants and many of these men had close links with St Ives.

The Bury–Stratton Trustees had to meet at least twice a year in St Ives and once a year in Potton, but by no means did all 178 men attend these meetings - a decision only required a majority vote amongst five Trustees. Most Turnpike Trusts were run by paid officials. These administrators, who were also Trustees, comprised a Clerk (who was often a lawyer), a Treasurer, and a Surveyor who supervised the road repairs. This system gave a reasonably efficient day to day running of the Trust, and allowed from the large cohort of Trustees, a generally indifferent participation at meetings.

The new Act extended the financial capacity of the Bury-Stratton Trust, allowing it to raise tolls and borrow £5000 (in addition to existing debts) to pay for the construction works:

> *And whereas a certain Part of the said Road commencing at the South End of a Street called Bridge Street in the Town of Saint Ives and leading over the Great Stone Bridge there, the length thereof being about Four Hundred and Forty Yards, is frequently overflowed with water, and at Times is impassable for Carriages; and His Grace the most Noble Duke of Manchester is liable to keep such part of the said Road as well as the said Bridge in Repair; and certain Tolls are collected, by or for the benefit of the said Duke..... And whereas such Part of the said Road might be improved, if Works were erected for the better Passage over the said Road in Times of Flood.... It shall be lawful for Five or more of the Trustees to enter into an Agreement with the said Duke for altering or repairing the said Road, and for the erecting of any Works...*

A Gentlemen's agreement

The Bury-Stratton Trust was proposing to reconstruct the road and, in particular, the causeway bridges which were owned and maintained by the Duke of Manchester; therefore the 1819 Act detailed the necessary agreements between the two parties.

The Trust was to build the new causeway and fund it through higher turnpike tolls. During this time the Duke of Manchester would suspend his toll to cross St Ives Bridge, and for this he would receive £50 per year in compensation. The period of higher turnpike tolls would last up to 18 years to allow the Trust to pay off all its building debts; after that the new causeway would become the property of the Duke and he would be responsible for its future maintenance

Who was the instigator of this plan to improve the causeway? Was it the Duke; after he failed to pass the expense of the road maintenance over to Hemingford Grey parish in 1810, had he then turned to the Turnpike Trust? Or had the Trust become so exasperated with constant disruptions to the road, and the difficulties of obtaining sufficient repairs from the Duke, that it decided to undertake the modernisation of the road across the flood meadow? Unfortunately the limited amount of remaining historical material does not answer these questions directly. However documents consistently show that expenditure on the Duchy estates was stringently controlled; it would appear that the Duke agreed to countenance the Trust's plan for a new causeway, solely because it would release him from the expense. And it is clearly evident that the Duke and his agents drove an extremely hard bargain. The building of the new causeway was only achieved after protracted, difficult negotiations where the Turnpike Trust had no option but to accept the Duke of Manchester's terms. The success of the Bury–Stratton road depended upon the river crossing at St Ives. The Trust needed travellers, and by 1820 travellers who paid tolls expected good roads.

Figs. 8 & 9 The Bury–Stratton turnpiked road, its tollgates and milestones

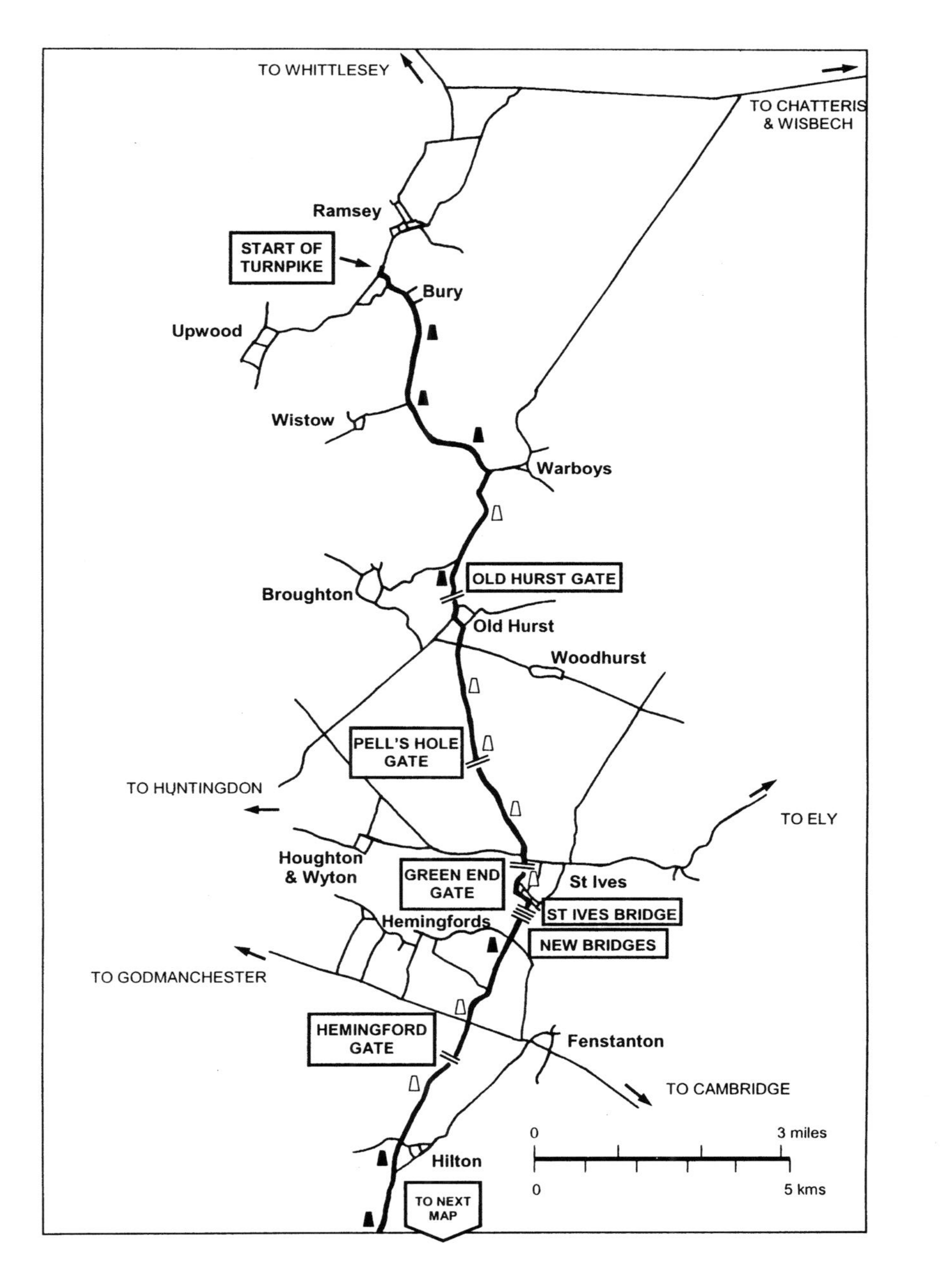

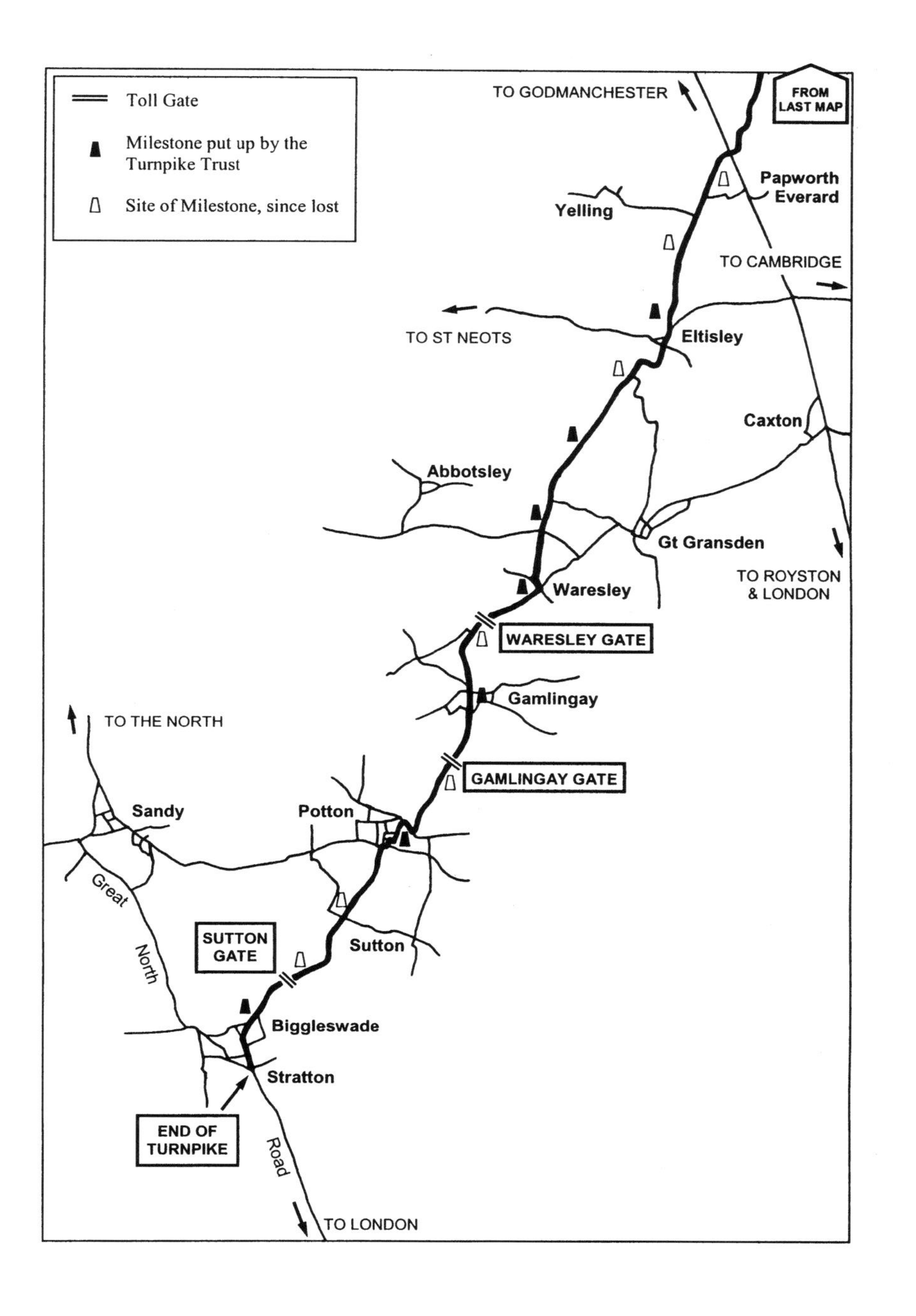

Toll Gate
Milestone put up by the Turnpike Trust
Site of Milestone, since lost
TO GODMANCHESTER
FROM LAST MAP
Papworth Everard
Yelling
TO CAMBRIDGE
TO ST NEOTS
Eltisley
Caxton
Abbotsley
Gt Gransden
TO ROYSTON & LONDON
Waresley
WARESLEY GATE
Gamlingay
TO THE NORTH
GAMLINGAY GATE
Sandy
Potton
Great North Road
SUTTON GATE
Sutton
Biggleswade
Stratton
END OF TURNPIKE
TO LONDON

A bad start to the new Act

As soon as the new Act came into force the Trust immediately raised the rate of tolls at all of its gates. The Trust was keen to accumulate funds for the planned road improvements, but, in direct contrast, the travelling public were understandably far from keen to pay higher tolls before they enjoyed such road improvements. There were strong objections to the increase and in response a meeting of the Trust had to be called for September 3rd 1819, *to consider the propriety of reducing the tolls*. The tolls were not reduced and another meeting was called on October 5th. The Trust decided to stand firm. Yet general dissatisfaction with the high prices continued and a third meeting had to be called where the Trustees were forced to consider, *making allowance to the several persons who have passed Stock or Cattle through the Gates during the increased rate of Toll.*

Division and turmoil within the Trust were revealed when a small group of Trustees succeeded in overturning the decisions of a previous meeting. The resulting debacle of contradictory decisions threatened the authority of the Trust and with it, public respect and confidence. Urgent arrangements had to be made to conduct business more strictly, *in order that a precedent (so fatal to the interest of the road) be not established, as empowering the Trustees of one Meeting to revoke or alter the Orders or Resolutions of a former Meeting without due notice being given of such intended Revocation or Alteration.*

But the matter of the raised tolls was not settled. Another meeting was called for November 23rd by Edward Theed, William Margetts, George Hewett, William Aislabbie and Thomas Allpress: *to take into consideration the propriety of rescinding so much of an Order of the Trustees made on the 2nd of July last, as relates to the toll for cattle with a view to reduce the same, it appearing to us that a loss has been sustained from the imposition of such a toll.* This group of Trustees were directly attributing a decline in livestock sales and inter-related business at St Ives Market to the rise in turnpike toll rates; they were successful in securing a vote for a reduction in the tolls:

> *TO DRIVERS OF BEASTS AND OTHER CATTLE.*
> *At a Meeting of the Trustees on Tuesday 18th January, after reducing part of the Tolls along the said Road, it was (amongst other things) Ordered that all Drovers of Oxen, Cows, Calves, or other neat Cattle, and Hogs, Swine, Goats, Sheep, or Lambs, who have passed the said Gates since the 3rd day of September last, and paid higher Tolls than those this day fixed may receive on application to Mr Matthew Wasdale of Saint Ives, the Treasurer to the said Trustees, part of the money so paid; and the Collectors at the several Toll Gates along the said Road are desired to give such information to the Drovers aforesaid, who intend to apply for the same, as will enable such drovers to make out their claim thereto.*

The public invitation to the drovers to claim toll refunds for three and a half months - a period which included the Michaelmas Fair, one of the largest cattle markets of the year - was a drastic situation for the Turnpike Trust. It could only have been prompted by exceptional circumstances. Furthermore, it must have been very embarrassing for the Trust to have its toll scheme reversed within six months of the new Act.

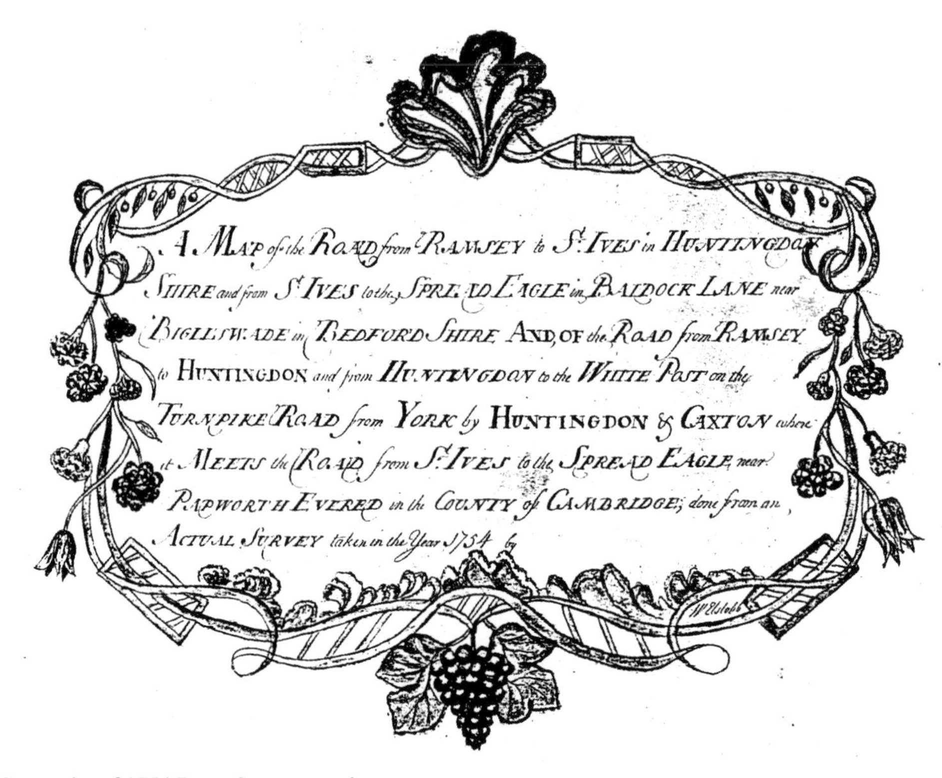

Fig. 10 Cartouche of 1754 Bury–Stratton road map
Elstobb enclosed the title of his map in a charming decoration of grapes, cherries, tulips and carnations.
The map was probably used as part of the application to Parliament for the original Private Act to turnpike the road. It would also have acted as an advertisement to potential trustees and investors; the map includes other main roads – Ramsey to Huntingdon, London to York via Royston, Caxton and Huntingdon, and Cambridge to Huntingdon. These links emphasised the commercial and economic benefits of the Bury-Stratton road.
County Record Office, Huntingdon Acc 1590

Bridges, Arches or other Works

Once the row over the tolls had subsided, the Trust was able to return to preparations for improving the road south of St Ives Bridge, but its financial plan of higher tolls to pay for the building works had sustained a severe blow - the projected income was now reduced. The Trust sought to repair this damage and requested authorisation *to borrow and take up interest on the Credit of the Tolls to be collected.* Turnpike Trusts could only raise capital by borrowing money against the surety of their toll income; this was because the Trusts managed the roads, they did not own them – the roads were 'the King's Highway'.

The Bury-Stratton Trust opened negotiations with the Duke. A meeting was called for February 15th 1820:

> *for the purpose of taking into consideration the propriety and expediency of endeavouring to enter into an Agreement with His Grace the Most Noble William Duke of Manchester.*

This endeavour must have been lengthy because no other notices about the proposed works appeared for well over a year. But in June 1821, the Trust appeared ready to proceed further, and an optimistic notice heralded the meeting:

> *A special meeting of the Trustees of the above Turnpike Road will be held at the Crown Inn, St Ives, on Friday the 13th day of July when a very full attendance of the Trustees of*

the said Turnpike Road and all other persons interested in the business to be discussed on that date, is most particularly requested, in order to take into consideration and determine on the propriety of erecting Arches along the said Turnpike Road between St Ives Bridge and Hailford, otherwise known as Helford Bridge, for the purpose of carrying off the waters in times of flood.

Friday 13th proved inauspicious - the meeting failed. The Trust's plans were rejected because it seems that, yet again, there was disagreement amongst the Trustees. Another meeting was quickly called to try to reverse the decision. Were those Trustees who opposed the building works concerned at the expense and financial viability of the project? Could they have been wary of the arrangements with the Duke of Manchester, or had someone dared to suggest that the Duke should build his own causeway? Or were there other reasons? We cannot be certain, but the Trust showed considerable determination to overcome the dissent; in time-honoured tradition, the disagreements of the meeting were dissolved by the appointment of a committee.

The next meeting on July 27th proved extremely effective when one of the Trustees, Mr John Margetts, offered to loan all the monies required for the new causeway - £5000 at 5% interest. The Margetts were a large, prosperous and influential family in Hemingford Grey, St Ives and Huntingdon. They were millers, merchants, farmers, brewers, and one William Margetts was a solicitor and Mayor of Huntingdon in 1813. John Margetts was well-known for his marriage in 1809 at Gretna Green to Sarah Gardner – soon after her marriage to George Ferrers Townshend, who became the Marquess of Townshend in 1811. Her inheritance, the Fordham estate in Cambridgeshire, had been entailed upon her marriage to Townshend. (This meant that the estate was legally bequeathed to her heirs and could not be sold.) But since she was not divorced Margetts ascribed his children with Sarah Gardner to the marquess, usurping the family titles. This was resolved by a Private Act of Parliament in 1843 (the year after Margetts' death) when the children were declared illegitimate. John Margetts lived in Brunswick Place, London from 1810, and his loan of £5000 shows that he was a man of considerable means.

John Margetts offered his loan on condition that the Trustees retained supervision of the construction work of the new causeway. His proposal was accepted by the meeting, and it was then agreed that he should find an *Engineer* to draw up plans for the new causeway. The Duke's Steward, Benjamin Welstead, was asked to attend the next meeting on August 21st when another committee was appointed *to treat with the Duke* – that is, draw up the necessary contracts between the Trust and the Duke. Mr Welstead insisted that the Duke should have his own representative oversee the building works, and nominated Mr William Ellis, a bricklayer from Kimbolton. The Trust appointed Mr William Biggs to be its Surveyor and, as Mr Margetts had stipulated, to be in overall charge of the works. Mr Biggs came from Linton in Cambridgeshire where Pigot's 1820 "Directory" lists him as *a joiner, builder, building surveyor and auctioneer.*

Once funds for the new causeway were secure, the Trust moved quickly. A meeting on August 21st resolved that the Trust would build the arches, and on August 23rd the financial arrangements with John Margetts were completed. An advertisement was placed in the Cambridge newspaper inviting tenders for the brickwork – *the quantity of Brickwork will be from 80 to 100 Rods.* The tenders were examined on August 31st, a builder chosen, contracts signed, and the Trust agreed that no building work should begin before April 2nd the following year.

At the same meeting, the details and measurements of the arches were revealed when the architect of the scheme *produced a plan.* It seems most probable that the architect was Mr Thomas Gwyn Elger of

Bedford – a builder of sufficient reputation and status as to be acceptable to both the Trust and the Duke. Mr Elger's father Isaac had been mayor of Bedford in 1802. After Isaac died Thomas was befriended by Samuel Whitbread, M.P. for Bedford, who, with the help of George Cloake a reputable architect, arranged him an apprenticeship in London. Thomas Gwyn Elger returned to Bedford and worked as a builder and designer; two examples of his work are Bedford Public Library and Biggleswade Union Workhouse. He was mayor of Bedford in 1830, 1835 and 1838. His younger brother Isaac was a surgeon and a close family friend of the Duchess of Bedford.

There are no surviving construction plans or drawings of the *Arches.* If the causeway had been a Public Utility there would have been a legal requirement for plans to be deposited in the House of Lords with the 1819 Act, but because the causeway was privately owned this was not necessary. Perhaps few drawings were done. We know that some drawings were brought to the meeting on August 31st 1821 in order to demonstrate the proposed new causeway to the Trustees and the Duke's agent. However a full plan of the New Bridges was not necessary for construction. Working drawings would only be required of a couple of sample arches rather than of all 55 arches; once the builder had the measurements of a standard arch, he and the surveyor could plan out the repetition of the rest.

Contemporary Causeways and Arches

In 1818 the Trust was planning to modernise a causeway that had hitherto remained essentially unchanged since medieval times. Around the country, other turnpike trusts who managed main roads had already undertaken engineering works to rebuild their old wooden and earth causeways.

The first causeway road scheme with multiple brick arches had been in Nottinghamshire, and its design probably became a model for other improvement works. A causeway carried the Great North Road, just north of Newark, across the flood plain between two branches of the River Trent almost a mile apart. This stretch of road was extremely busy with up to 90 coaches a day plus stage wagons and packhorses, but it regularly became impassable due to flooding. In 1766 the Turnpike Trustees had consulted John Smeaton a Fellow of the Royal Society and a renowned civil engineer of his day as the builder of the Eddystone Lighthouse. Smeaton made a detailed study of the floods and road, and designed a scheme comprising 72 brick arches each of 12 feet span, 9 tunnels and a raised road. He did not supervise the construction, and there were various alterations to his proposals – 87 arches and 8 tunnels - but it was completed in 1770 at a cost of £12,000. The largest group of arches that Smeaton designed was of 24 arches, although the largest to be built was of 18 arches. 'Smeaton's Arches', as they are still known today, were a great success and were acclaimed in an editorial note in the 1778 edition of Defoe's "A Tour Thro' the Whole Island of Great Britain":

> *the vast new-raised road over the flat often over-flowed by the Trent.... whether we consider the greatness or the utility of the work, it may be looked upon as one of the greatest of the kind ever executed in England.*

About five miles up-river from St Ives, at Godmanchester, there was the southern causeway to the Huntingdon Bridge - with historical similarities to St Ives; a medieval wooden causeway, with recurring maintenance disputes, was rebuilt in 1784 by the Royston to Wansford Bridge Turnpike Trust who managed part of the national route of 'Ermine Street' – London to York. It is highly likely that the new

Fig. 11 Cook's Bridge, Godmanchester
These eight brick arches are part of the causeway to Huntingdon Bridge, built in 1784 by the Royston-Wansford Bridge Turnpike Trust. The bridge was sympathetically repaired and strengthened by Cambridgeshire County Council in 2001.

Fig. 12 A section of 'Smeaton's Arches', carrying the old Great North Road north of Newark
This important piece of mid 18th century engineering has suffered from the demands of 20th century traffic. When the road was widened in 1922, nearly all the brick arches were demolished on one side and rebuilt in concrete. Some of the sets of arches were later demolished to make way for a roundabout. A phased programme of refurbishment and internal strengthening of the remaining arches and their brickwork was carried out by Nottinghamshire County Council in the 1980s. The A1 now runs on a dual carriageway by-pass to the east of Newark.

causeway at Godmanchester was much admired in St Ives, but it was to be over 35 years before the Bury-Stratton Trust was to achieve the same. The Godmanchester causeway comprised a raised embankment and two eight-arched brick bridges; the embanked road is still there today but only one of the bridges, known as 'Cook's Bridge' after a 17th century benefactor, remains.

Further south in Bedfordshire there were two sets of seven flood arches either side of Tempsford Bridge across the River Great Ouse. The river bridge, which still carries the northbound A1 road, was rebuilt in 1820 and the causeway arches added, not by the turnpike trust responsible for that part of the Great North Road, but by the local Quarter Sessions. The arches are built in brick with stone facings and parapet.

The causeway to Bromham Bridge, also in Bedfordshire over the River Great Ouse, was rebuilt in 1814 with 21 stone arches, but although it looked very fine, it almost immediately required constant repair and in 1850 the County Surveyor reported that *a worse constructed Bridge, and with worse Materials, could not have been built.*

An ambitious undertaking

The scale of the new causeway at St Ives was considerable in comparison to what it was to replace; it was also impressive in relation to contemporary schemes. The Bury-Stratton Trustees had decided that a viaduct across the whole flood plain was necessary to secure their road above flood level. And they would have been aware that the building of a 55 arched causeway was a very expensive, ambitious and unprecedented undertaking for a small, rural Turnpike Trust.

The building of a new causeway to St Ives Bridge was driven purely by economic necessity - if the town did not have the modern facilities for business, then that business would go elsewhere. This threat promised to become reality when, in October 1821, within weeks of the Trust having signed the bricklaying contracts for the causeway, the Mayor of Huntingdon's plans for his coming year of office were reported in the local newspaper:

The new mayor seems anxious to confer one solid benefit upon the town...the establishment of a stock market, which, if it succeeds, is intended to be continued weekly. We understand this has long been desired by the northern graziers, as the site is more convenient to them than St Ives to which place Huntingdon has hitherto been but a resting place; where if they can dispose of their stock, a material saving of expense will accrue.

These words must have concentrated minds in St Ives. The town had much to lose: Pigot's 1830 "Directory" described the St Ives Monday corn and cattle market as being:

with the exception of Smithfield, the largest cattle market in the kingdom.

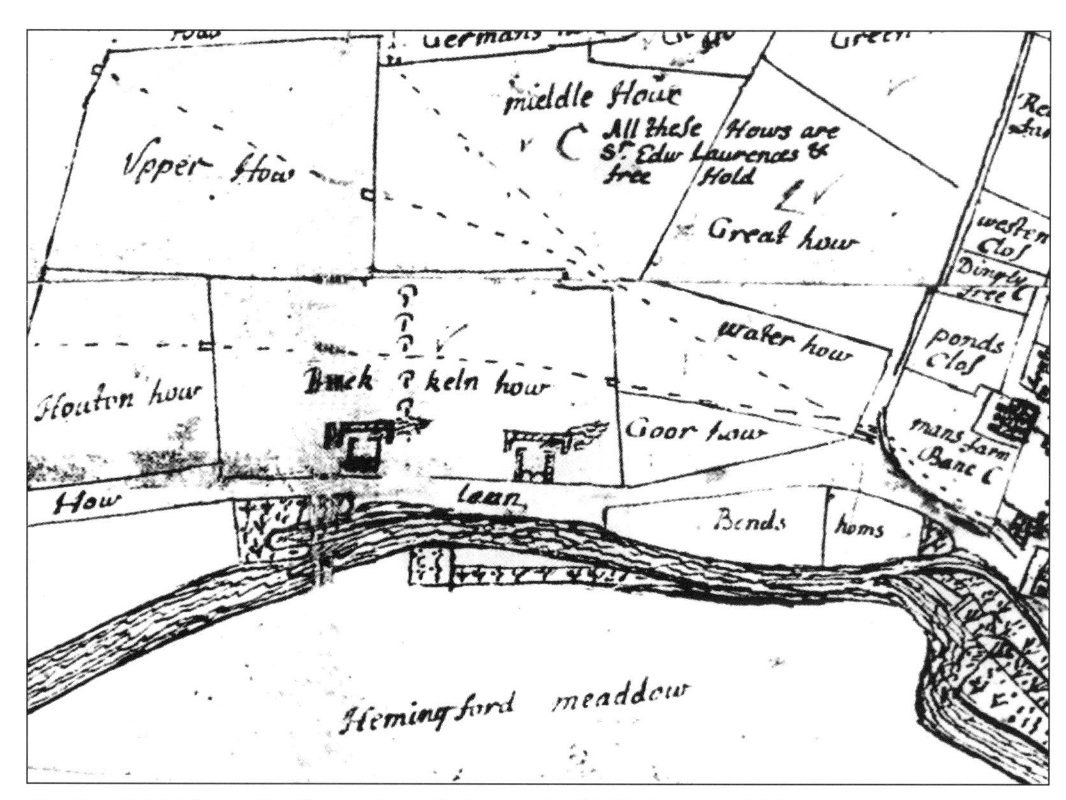

Fig.13 Brick kilns at The How as shown in Edmund Pettis' 1728 survey of St Ives

In his detailed maps Pettis' simple drawings, along with his individual spelling, contain significant amounts of information. At the bottom of "Brick keln how" alongside "How lean" (today's Thicket Path), two kilns (or clamps) are shown being fired; there are fire holes at the bottom of the clamps, and flames and smoke issuing from the top. On a similar map Pettis drew the hacks where the unfired bricks were left to dry before firing.

Norris Museum

The building of 'The Great White Bridge'

At last, almost four years after the first announcement of the new causeway project in 1818, building was about to begin. Tenders were invited for the foundation work:

> *To CARPENTERS and others, Notice is hereby given, that the Trustees of the Bury and Stratton Turnpike Road are desirous to CONTRACT and agree with any Person or Persons for laying down Planking on Sleepers for the foundations of such Arches or other Works, and also for excavating foundations for the same Planking.*

The advertisement appeared on March 27th 1822; specifications were available on March 30th and bids had to be received by 11.00 a.m. on Friday April 5th - the earliest possible starting date was Monday April 8th. No time was to be wasted. The construction teams needed to use the optimum weather conditions of spring and summer, and the Trust had drawn up tough contracts to ensure that the causeway was completed as fast as possible - delays would affect the income of the Trust, the town and the market.

Mr Biggs, as the man in charge, had a huge organisational task, and he would have begun by preparing the construction site. Before he could demolish the old causeway and its bridges he needed to lay down a temporary road in order to maintain access to St Ives. Then he had to build some form of quay on the inlet channel of the river parallel to the western side of the New Bridges - where there is now a ditch beside the Dolphin Hotel. This channel may have already existed, or may have been specifically cut by the builders, but it was very important because it allowed the vast quantities of timber, bricks and mortar to be brought by barge to the construction site. Finally, Mr Biggs needed to make arrangements for his work force. If the labourers were not local, they needed to be lodged in the town or in camps set up around the site.

Bricks and mortar

The new causeway was to be built of bricks made in St Ives. (There was no source of stone local to St Ives which meant that transport costs alone would have made stone prohibitively expensive). Skeeles gives details of the bricks:

> *The edge of the How Hill from Houghton to St Ives, the site of The Thicket included, shows traces of the digging of clay for brick making. The 'How' brickyard provided bricks during the 19th century. It was said to have furnished bricks for the New Bridges conveyed by boats via the River and meadow ditch close to the work.*

The financial benefits and logistical advantages of being able to float the bricks less than half a mile downstream from the brickyards to the construction site were vital to the success of the project. Indeed, the viability of the whole scheme may have depended upon it.

The How Hill brickyards (the site of today's St Ives Golf Course, in particular Number Eight fairway and green) had produced brown–red bricks from the surface clays but these were exhausted in the 18th century. By the 19th century, clay was being extracted from the lower levels at the How and this clay produced very hard, pale coloured bricks as Skeeles describes: *white bricks began to be made from lower beds of clay*. In 1823 there are four references to the New Bridges being called 'The Great White Bridge'.

Lime mortar was used in the bricklaying. Skeeles describes how limestone or 'clunch' was burnt in kilns to produce lime:

> *Lime burning was carried on by Mr James Fields at his yard below the bridge, and Mr Samuel Dore Ulph on the Ramsey Road, and Messrs Lindsell also owned a kiln. The kilns were of brick, circular and bottle-shaped, with openings for charging, firing and clearing. The [lime] stone was brought up to St Ives by barges, and the coal also.*

To make a mortar, the lime was 'slaked' by adding water, then mixed with proportions of sand and coarse material and left to mature in specially dug lime pits for several weeks before use.

The tops of the parapet walls of the new causeway were to be handsomely finished in stone on both sides of the 700 feet long causeway. Tenders were invited:

> *Stone Masons. Stone Coping; the quantity of work required to be done on the Line of Works is about one thousand four hundred feet run.*

How many bricks, and how were they made?

Brick-making in the early 19th century was grindingly hard work. In his history of brick-making, "Bricks to build a House", John Woodforde summarises:

> *Few occupations were thought meaner than brickmaking and few kinds of workmen rougher than those who followed it.*

Clay was hand-dug by spade in the autumn and then left in heaps over the winter to be 'weathered', as exposure to the frosts helped to break down the stiff, greasy lumps. In the spring the clay was 'tempered'- that is trodden or turned with *spade labour* before being thrown into a 'pug mill', a large mixing barrel in which the clay was kneaded with ground chalk, ashes and water to produce an even consistency. A horse turned the pug mill, and it was reckoned that if a horse walked around for ten hours per day, 12 cubic yards of clay could be prepared, and that was sufficient for about 6000 bricks. Every brick was hand made. Clay was pressed into a sand-lined mould and then turned out onto a pallet – a process known as slip or pallet moulding. An experienced moulder, with assistants – usually children - first bringing him the clay and then lifting the moulded bricks off his bench, could produce 4000 bricks in a 12 hour day from 6.00 a.m. to 6.00 p.m. This team needed a further two men to wheelbarrow the bricks and place them on low racks called 'hacks' for drying for up to six weeks. When the bricks were half dry they would be 'scintled' or placed further apart to ensure they dried evenly. The 'green' bricks were fired in a clamp, or temporary kiln which burnt for about 3-5 weeks and contained up to 120,000 bricks. After firing the kiln was dismantled, and the bricks graded for quality; the best to be used for facing work on the building, the lesser quality being used as infill, whilst up to 30% of the kiln's production was waste and would be used to build a new kiln.

How many bricks were made for the New Bridges? The advertised tender estimated *80 – 100 rods of brickwork.* A rod of brickwork is 272 square yards of bricks. The number of bricks in a square yard is determined by the size of brick and the thickness of mortar joint. With bricks of the dimensions 9" x 2¾" making 47 to each square yard it is calculated that there are about 1,250,000 – 1,300,000 bricks in the New Bridges. A stockpile of bricks must have been accumulated in anticipation of construction of the New Bridges.

The bridge builder

The only record of the builder of the New Bridges is on the stone plaque on the western wall of the bridge; its inscription is now so eroded that it is barely legible, but it has been noted that it once read, *John Turner 1822.* Very little is known about John Turner, except that in 1820 he was a bricklayer from King Street, and in 1830, Maid's Causeway, Cambridge.

Inscriptions on bridges often refer to a benefactor who endowed the building, but there was certainly no philanthropy involved in the building of the New Bridges; it was strictly a commercial enterprise. John Turner may have contracted to have his name placed on the bridge as a form of advertisement. The bridge was owned by the Duke of Manchester and any inscriptions would have needed his permission. Hence the name of the Bury-Stratton Turnpike Trust was omitted – the Duke would not have wanted the Trust's name on his bridge. Whilst the Duke refrained from putting his own name on the bridge, he must have agreed that the 55 arched causeway was worthy of recognition and that a simple plaque could mark the bridge's builder and date of completion.

Fig. 14 John Turner 1822
The inscription for John Turner - the man who built the New Bridges - will soon be gone. This photograph was taken over ten years ago; today the carving is even more eroded, so that virtually nothing is legible.

Many men at work

When construction began, progress was rapid - the new causeway was built in just over 23 weeks. This speed seems astonishing. But the working days would have been long; there are records of a bridge being built in Essex in 1785 where the bricklayers worked in shifts covering 3.00 a.m. until midnight, and being paid double time on Sundays.

Work probably started at the St Ives end of the road and moved south. The ground workers began; they excavated the meadow soil for a hard surface on the gravels. As levels were checked and alignments made by the surveyors, the heavy wooden sleepers were laid for the base of the foundations. Carpenters followed, and built a 'mattress' of planking on top of the sleepers. The construction of the brick arches then began. The time schedule was such that the arches were probably built not individually, but two or three or more at a time, with the bricklayers and carpenters working in parallel gangs. The carpenters constructed timber 'centrings' to form the arches and then, when the arches had been built in brick and the mortar sufficiently hardened, the timber frames were taken down and moved on to where the next arches were to be built. Flat brick inverts were laid as flooring for the arches, and stone coping topped the parapet walls. This whole production line was probably generating three finished arches each week.

It is a pity (and surprising) that there are no surviving first-hand accounts in letters or diaries of the building work in 1822; the whole event must have been a remarkable sight for St Ives.

Fig. 15 'View of St Ives, Huntingdonshire, from How Hill' by R. Harraden 1802
Although this is a 'view of St Ives', the How brickyards are in the forefront of this engraving. Harraden may have been emphasising the importance of the How brickmaking industry in relation to St Ives. The exposed banks show where clay has been dug, and there are piles of clay near the sheds. Men are seen building a clamp. They are pushing open-sided 'hack barrows' – wheel barrows specifically designed to carry bricks.
Norris Museum, St Ives *PWD/S.IVE/25*

BRICK-KILNS
SAINT IVES, HUNTS

To be LET by AUCTION
By JOHN REMINGTON

On WEDNESDAY the 9th day of October instant, at the *Golden Lion*, in *St Ives*, between the hours of six and eight in the evening, for the term of Seven Years from the 11th October inst:

All those old-established BRICK-KILNS situate in ST. IVES, adjoining the River Ouze navigable from Lynn to Bedford and Cambridge, containing 15A. (more or less) of superior Brick Earth now in the occupation of Mr. JOHN MARGETTS, who is retiring from business.

The situation of these Kilns, and the long-established custom thereto, demands the attention of any one wishing to withdraw his capital from farming and to employ it in trade, as any quantity may be made and conveyed away by water, and the present occupier has this year sold off the same ground above TWELVE HUNDRED THOUSAND BRICKS.

For a view of the premises apply to BEASLEY SUMMERS, who is at work thereon.

N.B. – On the same evening will be LET by AUCTION, TWO LOTS of excellent GRAZING LAND, one containing 30A. and the other 4A; to be entered on the 11th of October inst.

Fig. 16 John Margetts and the How Brickyards
Cambridge Chronicle, October 4th 1822

This advertisement reveals just how closely John Margetts was involved in the building of the New Bridges. Not only did he finance the project and find the design engineer, he also contracted with the Trustees to sell them all the bricks from his brickmaking business at the How. Earlier records show that his younger brother William had been the lessee of the How. He had died in 1818 and it is probable that the tenancy was passed to John. He kept the lease only until the New Bridges were built; within three weeks of their completion, the advertisement for the new lease boasted of the 1.2 million bricks used in the New Bridges.

Fig 17 View of St Ives from the Golf Club in 2005

In 1923 St Ives (Hunts) Golf Club was formed and 55 acres of land known as 'The Brick Hills' were bought for £2250. This site of the old brickyards on the slopes of the How Hill was ideal for a nine hole golf course; very little landscaping other than the creation of greens was necessary because of the irregular contours and banks left from the clay diggings. The steeper faces of the clay workings have been left as wild areas - either ponds or now grown up with shrubs. In very dry years such as 1976 and 2003 the extensive outlines of the brick clamps could be seen along the Number Eight fairway which is near the Thicket Path. These earth marks revealed long, narrow rectangular shapes (as shown in Harraden's drawing in Fig. 15) The clamps were obviously sited near to the river for the convenience of transport – both of fuel and the finished bricks; they were built on a general east/west axis so that the fires would benefit from the prevailing wind. Some of the 55 acres were later compulsorily purchased by the Local Authority for St Ivo School and the Recreation Centre.

A Grand Opening 17th September 1822

Celebrations were in order for the opening ceremony of the new causeway. The Wisbech coach, drawn by six horses rather than the customary four, led the procession. "The Independent Press" described the scene:

> *On Tuesday last, the new bridge, or road on arches, erected by the Trustees of the Potton Road, at the London entrance to the town of St Ives, was opened for public use. The Wisbech coach, drawn by six horses, and preceded by a band of music, passed over; witnessed by a numerous and respectable assemblage, whom the novelty of the scene had collected together. The bridge is a plain brick structure consisting of fifty eight arches. A handsome dinner was provided on the occasion, by Mrs Bricheno at the Dolphin Inn, of which upwards of 50 gentlemen partook – Thomas Lindsell Esq. in the Chair. Several patriotic toasts and songs were then given, and the evening was spent in the greatest harmony; excepting a slight difference of opinion as to the name to be given to the bridge, which we understand, is to be settled on a future occasion.*

A name for the causeway was obviously never agreed. *The new bridge* became "The New Bridges". It is interesting that the newspaper reporter enthusiastically counted 58 arches instead of 55 – he was the first, but certainly not the last, to make mistakes in counting the many arches of the New Bridges.

The Trust held a meeting for the 'signing off' of the building contract on December 27th 1822 and *for the purpose of inspecting and adjusting the accounts of building the Arches near Saint Ives, and receiving the final Report of the Committee for that purpose.* The original contract had stipulated that the builders would not be fully paid until both the Trust and the Duke were satisfied with the work. Skeeles' firm was employed to survey the completed New Bridges for this final report, and a note from George Skeeles' journal of December 12th 1822 describes the payment to his men for *measuring brickwork for J. Burford, T. Mason, E. Saint.*

Fig. 18 The Wisbech coach
This contemporary engraving shows the Wisbech coach, called 'The Day', pulled up alongside the Forty Foot Drain near Chatteris to watch a famous skating match in 1823.
Norris Museum, St Ives *PH/SKATE/01*

A Toll Gate for the New Bridges

The New Bridges had cost £4345-7s-6d to build. A hidden, but significant part of this cost was the tax on bricks; this tax had been introduced in 1784 to pay for the American War of Independence, but was not repealed until 1850. Bricks were taxed at the rate of five shillings per thousand in 1822. The tax was levied on the brickmakers, and, if paid, on 1,300,000 bricks for the New Bridges amounted to £325. In addition to the building costs there was also the accumulating interest on the borrowed capital; the agreed term of John Margetts' loan is not known. But in order to repay the capital plus interest, the Trust had to increase its revenue, and so it planned to create another toll gate.

In seeking to maximise toll income, but minimise public criticism, the Trust felt that a toll gate on the New Bridges would be acceptable to travellers enjoying the benefits of the splendid new causeway. It was explained that this toll gate would not be permanent; it would be taken down when its receipts had paid for the building of the New Bridges. Furthermore, the Trust argued, a turnpike gate on the New Bridges was merely a temporary substitute for the Duke's St Ives Bridge toll. But the public felt, as now, that although tax came in many forms, it was always a burden.

The 1819 Act had allowed for eight turnpike toll gates along the Bury-Stratton road, but there were only six in place - Old Hurst, Green End, Hemingford (sometimes called Hilton), Waresley, Gamlingay, and Sutton. Two of the turnpike toll gates were north of St Ives and four were to the south. During 1819, whilst the first row over raised tolls had been raging, the Trustees had decided to move one of the northern toll gates and place it in a more strategic position to increase its revenue. This was the Pell's Hole Gate and it became the St Ives Green End Gate. In its new position, just south of the cross roads of the Bury road

(Ramsey Road) and the Huntingdon-Ely road (St Audrey's Way) it could collect payment from all travellers entering and leaving St Ives. Once again, a plan that seemed commercial good sense to the Trust was resented by the public who saw it as the noose of taxation being drawn ever more tightly. But on that occasion the Trustees had been resolute; in 1819 they moved the Pell's Hole Gate to Green End, near to today's 'Seven Wives' pub.

In 1823 matters were not to be so straightforward. It took four meetings between January and March 1823, with vacillating decisions, before it was agreed that the Trust would build a seventh toll gate, with a house for its keeper, on the New Bridges – close to today's entrance to the Dolphin Hotel car park.

Inevitably, there was another row. The public objected strongly to an increase in the cost of travel and lobbied the Creditors of the Trust. The Creditors held a key position; they could exert pressure upon the Trust to ensure that their loans, plus interest, were secure, or if matters were not to their satisfaction they could threaten to withdraw their funds and potentially bankrupt the Trust. (In practice they would only withdraw their money in exceptional circumstances because the Turnpike Trusts generally offered about half to three-quarters per cent higher interest than elsewhere.) The Clerk called a meeting for May 6th 1823: *to ascertain the result of the application about to be made to the Creditors of the said Turnpike Road as to REDUCING the TOLLS, as now taken at the newly erected Bar, near the lately erected Arches. And also then and there to fix the rate of the Toll hereafter, to be taken agreeably to the consent of the said Creditors.* After considerable pressure the Trust bowed to the protesters and offered a compromise - the New Bridge Gate would remain, but its level of toll would be reduced. This caused a ferocious new argument, because the tolls at the New Bridge Gate were then half the price of those at all the other gates along the Bury-Stratton road.

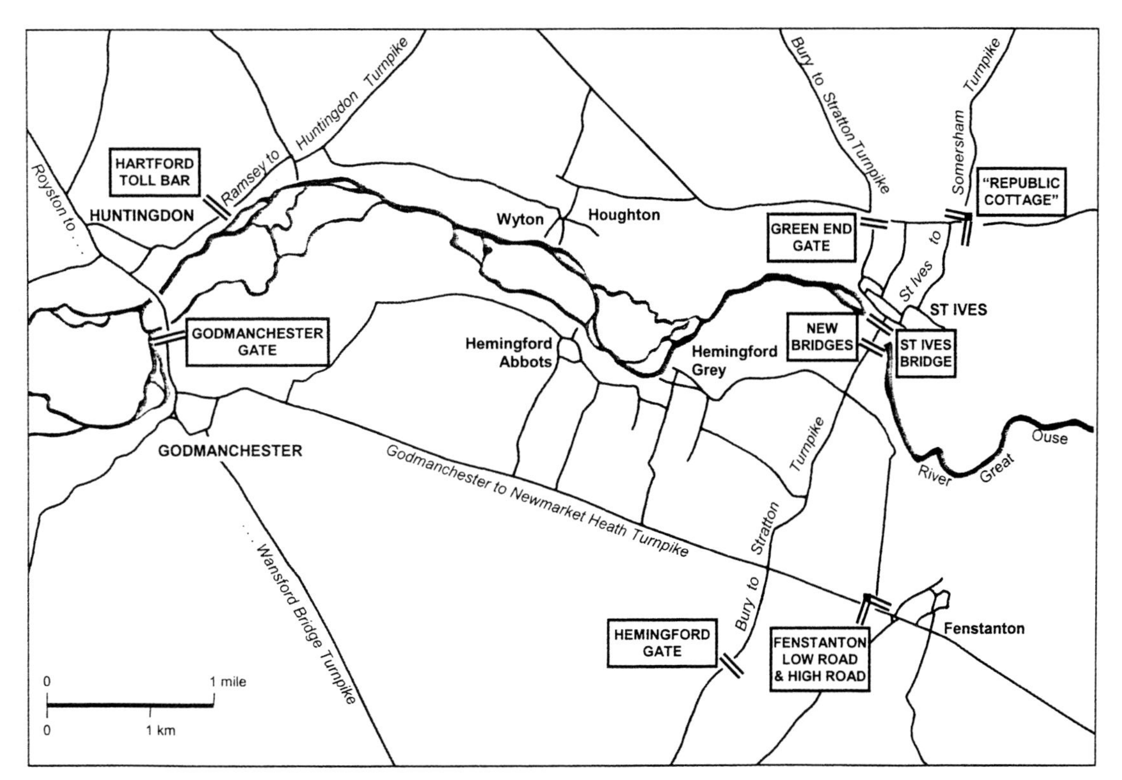

Fig. 19 The Toll gates around St Ives

All the main roads around Huntingdon and St Ives were turnpiked in the 18th century. Each Trust placed its toll gates at strategically important sites along its road; several of these sites were adjacent to the two main river crossings at St Ives and Huntingdon and, as a consequence, St Ives in particular was encircled by toll gates. The Trusts also erected side gates along their roads to prevent anyone taking a diversion to escape payment of the tolls.

Coach travel along the local turnpike roads in 1815 and 1825

HUNTINGDON and CAMBRIDGE
NEW COACH,
THE BLUCHER,

SETS out from the GEORGE INN, HUNTINGDON, every Morning at Nine o'Clock, by the way of St. Ives, to the

PICKERELL INN, CAMBRIDGE;

From whence are conveyances to London, Lynn, Bury and Oxford; returns every day at Half-past One and arrives at Huntingdon at Four o'Clock, where it meets Coaches immediately to Peterborough, Stamford, and the North.

WM. EVERETT, Proprietor.

Who will not be accountable for any Package whatever, above the value of 5l. if lost, unless entered as such, and paid for accordingly.

Fig. 20 Coach advertisement, July 1815
The coach journey from Cambridge to Huntingdon, via St Ives, took two and a half hours. The coach was named 'The Blucher' after the Prussian General Blücher – one of the heroes of the battle of Waterloo in June that year.
The Huntingdon, Bedford and Peterborough Gazette, & Independent Press, July 1815

Fig 21 A crash at the Fenstanton Clock Tower

Journey by coach could be dangerous. A frightening collision was reported in the newspaper.:

> "On Wednesday morning a serious accident occurred to the Boston mail between Cambridge and this place (Huntingdon). On reaching within a mile of Fenstanton, where the change takes place, the horses, from being alarmed, or some other cause, started at full speed, and becoming quite unmanageable, passed the inn where they usually stop, at a furious rate, until their progress was impeded by coming into contact with the clockhouse, which fronts the road at that place, with great violence; and but for the fortunate circumstance of one of the wheels becoming tight locked with a railing in front of the building, the coach must have been dashed to pieces, and the most serious consequences might have been the result to the passengers."

The Huntingdon, Bedford and Peterborough Gazette, & Independent Press, July 2nd 1825

Letters to the Editor

The argument over the St Ives New Bridge Gate tolls moved into the newspapers. In the 1820s local news for Huntingdon and St Ives could be found in two papers: "The Cambridge Chronicle" and "The Huntingdon, Bedford and Peterborough Gazette, and Cambridge and Hertford Independent Press". These weekly newspapers had a significant difference in style and, very importantly, in their politics. "The Chronicle" was High Tory - supporting King and Constitution. It was a County paper with advertisements, notices and social engagements, but very few local reports. "The Independent Press" contained less copy from the national papers, and much more local news than "The Chronicle". It had solid support for Dissenters and moderate reformers, and although it gradually became more openly radical, it managed to retain support from the local Whigs. The weekly circulation figure for "The Independent Press" has been calculated for 1833 as being about 1700 with a probable readership of ten to twelve times that number. In his book "Cambridge Newspapers and Opinion 1780-1850", Michael Murphy describes the two papers:

> *"The Independent Press" was a staunchly non-conformist organ. It opposed the privileges of the Church of England and supported the demands for civil and religious equality. On major reform questions, both local and national, "The Independent Press" stimulated political awareness by encouraging debate and discussion. County meetings, election speeches and events were fully reported, usually accompanied by editorial comments. The overwhelming characteristic of "The Chronicle" was its Tory parochialism and commitment to the status quo.*

"The Chronicle" published only a selection of the public notices relating to the Bury-Stratton Trust's meetings whereas "The Independent Press" published them all. News items, letters and editorials about the Trust featured solely in "The Independent Press".

When the editor of "The Independent Press", Mr Weston Hatfield of Huntingdon, printed the first letter about the New Bridge tolls, readers may have felt that it seemed to raise pertinent questions about a controversial issue – the price of travel; the Bury-Stratton Turnpike Trust had held many meetings in the previous four years about the level of their tolls. But, as Hatfield knew, the 1823 complaints over the tolls at the New Bridges, whilst appearing similar to previous arguments, were different, and very complicated. When the replies to the original letter were printed, the readers would have realised (if they did not know it already) that the protagonists were not concerned with the suffering of the over-taxed traveller. Two factions of the Trustees were arguing over Trust policy; an intransigent old gentleman and his supporters were quarrelling with the businessmen of St Ives. The profile of this argument was significantly raised by the correspondence to "The Independent Press" in 1823. It became a public spectacle when the tournament of letters gathered momentum and considerable damage was inflicted on both sides.

A great deal is said in your paper concerning this road...

"The Independent Press" published a total of six letters from three writers. Initially the writers chose the customary style of anonymity, whilst hinting at their identity with a partially disguised signature. Local newspaper readers would have endeavoured to unmask the players – *'Circumnavigator', 'A Trustee'* and

'A Creditor'. Mr G. G. Hewett signed his name to his September letter because by then everyone knew he was *'Circumnavigator'*. The letters were formal but not restrained. For example *'A Creditor'* said that *'Circumnavigator'*: *should quit the field and return to his proper element - marine roads.*

After *'Circumnavigator'* likened the Trustees to: *a herd of banditti,* 'A Trustee' replied that he: *hoped numbers will incline on the side of reason without the aid of pistols.*

Mr Hewett threatened: *to give them such a broadside of truths, as shall make them strike their black flags as quickly as other pirates, or other enemies of Britain.*

'Circumnavigator' began the correspondence; he took the high moral ground against the injustice of unequal tolls, and led a rallying call for the New Bridge Gate tolls to be the same rate as the tolls at the other gates along the Bury-Stratton road. The letters from *'A Trustee'* and *'A Creditor'* were stalwart defences of the Trust's policies, and tried to counteract the unfavourable public image of Trust infighting caused by Mr Hewett.

Letter from *'A Trustee'*, April 26th 1823

> *...In order to defray the expenses of erecting these works a toll-gate has been erected near thereto, and it is proposed that such toll shall be of sufficient extent to enable the trustees to pay the interest of the debt created by the charges of erecting the said works, the £50 per annum to his Grace the Duke of Manchester; and also to enable the trustees to provide a sufficient fund to discharge the debt so incurred; and that when those objects are*

performed the toll shall cease. If this proposition is carried into effect the public will have a good and commodious road in lieu of a road impassible in times of flood or nearly so, and the money paid for the ferry boats amounting in some seasons to upwards of £150, and the losses occasioned by stock being drowned or otherwise injured in passing over the water which may be estimated at £150, will be saved, and the payment for such accommodation will be a small toll in addition to the amount heretofore paid to his Grace, and that during the operation of this act – only a period of about 18 years. …

Letter from 'Circumnavigator', May 3rd 1823
…his proposition of a small toll for his own town, and a large one for every other on the same trust, is a measure never attempted or heard on any other road; and to prevent so great a piece of injustice being carried into execution is my chief reason for thinking the attendance of every impartial trustee necessary at the meeting to be held on 6th May.

After allowing his readers the detailed exchange of views in the five letters printed in April and May, the editor of the newspaper himself then chose to speak on the subject of excessive turnpike tolls. It is uncertain if many readers were able to follow his described itinerary in the paradise of non-turnpiked northern England, but his message was clear - travel in the County of Huntingdon was far too expensive:

Such is the state of the roads in the North Riding of Yorkshire (and wholly maintained by the townships) that people may travel on horseback, or in carriages, from Whitby to

Stockton, and Yarm, also from Whitby to Skelton Castle, Upleatham, Kirkleatham, Wilton Castle, Ormsby Park, and westward from Gainsborough in a direct line to Ayton, Stokesley, Cleveland Tontine Inn, Northallerton, Bedale, Masham, Hornby and Bolton Castle, Jerveaux Abbey, Middleham, Leyburn, Aysgarth, Askrigg, the whole of Wensleydale, and further westwards towards Lancashire, with the glorious certainty of not having to pay so much as a single turnpike gate on the whole line of road. But if we poor Huntingdon folks desire but to go to Ely, a distance of 21 miles, with a single pair of horses, must pay tolls to the amount of between 4 and 5 shillings, or three pence per mile.

No doubt the travelling public agreed with the editor, and wished they could live in North Yorkshire.

The combination of the two letters printed in one edition on May 24th 1823 represented the might of the Trust in a furious attack on *'Circumnavigator'* for his meddlesome behaviour:

The Trustees of this road have for a long period conducted the operations of this trust without such imputations, and will continue to do so without regarding the tone of dictation assumed by him.

Litigation looms

Mr Hewett was undeterred by the personal criticisms, and instead seemed to relish the publicity for what he saw as his crusade for justice against the tyranny of the Trust. His last letter of September 1st 1823 signed as 'Mr G Hewett, Hilton', contained an undisguised threat of legal action:

A great deal has been said in your paper concerning this road, and being a Trustee, I do not wish to have any share in the honour due to those who, made an order, that a smaller toll should be taken near St Ives than at any other bar between that place and Biggleswade. I therefore take this method of saying that I have done and will persevere in doing the duties of an impartial trustee, by opposing and endeavouring to set aside that order, which I am certain I can convince any man of sense who has a spark of honour, or a character to lose, is a most unjustifiable one, and if not also illegal.

Mr George Goodman Hewett was a surgeon who lived at Hilton Hall, and history has remembered him as an especially litigious man. Jack Dady in "Hilton, Huntingdonshire" describes him: *as the scourge of those in Hilton who transgressed the law.* In 1827 Mr Hewett had the village constable prosecuted and fined £2 because of an administrative error. In 1828, when he quarrelled with a neighbour over the siting of a well, the village constable incited the locals to sing the refrain:

The Devil's dead, all Hell will rue it,
His friend succeeds him, G. G. Hewett,
Alas poor Hilton, how you'll rue it
If you are governed by G.G. Hewett.

Mr Hewett was not amused, and sued the constable for libel, having him fined £5 and bound over to keep the peace for a year. Mr Hewett next queried the churchwarden's accounts, which so outraged the churchwarden that a fight ensued between them in the churchyard. Mr Hewett was left bleeding amongst the tombstones for which the churchwarden, Mr Peck, was fined £20.

The Great Flood of 1823

Later that year in November, there was the biggest flood in living memory (although the flood of 1797 was reputed to have been very high). Such a flood must have been the answer to many a Trustee's prayers; the building of the New Bridges was clearly vindicated. The newspaper gave a graphic description:

> *THE OVERFLOW OF THE OUSE – Never in the memory of man has the water risen so high and never has its course been more destructive. Almost from its source in Buckinghamshire to the very meeting of the tide, the country through which it flows is laid desolate, inundating entire towns and villages, sweeping away flocks and herds and in many instances human beings; while every description of property has suffered.*
> *ST IVES – About noon on Sunday, when the flood was at the highest, the Bullock Market [the present-day Broadway] was completely inundated as far up as the Cow and Hare and boats were provided for the conveyance of such of the inhabitants as had courage to brave the waters to and from church. ......*
> *The family at the New Toll House erected in the road between St Ives and Fenstanton, to*

collect the tolls for the new archway, were thrown into considerable alarm by the rising of the water which completely inundated their little dwelling; and having no upper floor to resort to, the distress of Staples, the collector, his wife and children, can be more readily imagined than described. They remained in a most deplorable condition, knee deep in water, for several hours, before they could contrive to make their situation known at St Ives, whence a boat was afterwards dispatched for their relief. As a proof of the unprecedented height of the waters, the spot on which this house was erected was selected for the purpose, as never having been, from its elevated position, affected by the floods.

Fig. 22 The toll house at the Sutton Gate
The Sutton Gate toll house was the longest surviving turnpike toll house along the Bury-Stratton road; it was demolished in the 1970s to make way for road widening. The little toll house had windows on either side so that the keeper could watch for approaching travellers. Inside there could not have been space for more than two rooms; living conditions for the keeper and his family must have been cramped. The original toll house on the New Bridges was most probably of the same design as this toll house at the Sutton Gate. Behind the toll house is 'Turnpike Farm'.
County Record Office, Bedford PU78/1967 no3

The Huntingdon,
Bedford, and Peterborough
GAZETTE.

"Nothing extenuate,
" Nor set down aught in malice."
SHAKESPEARE.

HUNTINGDON.

Fig. 23 The title of "The Huntingdon Gazette" within "The Independent" newspaper
Its admirable motto was : "Nothing extenuate, Nor set down aught in malice."

Mr Hewett's Revenge

Mr Hewett's campaign of letters was unsuccessful. When he failed to persuade sufficient Trustees to vote against the New Bridge tolls, he did as he had promised, and in 1824 turned to the law to prove his case. He gave evidence to the Magistrates at the Huntingdon Quarter Sessions that the tolls being taken at the New Bridge Gate were illegal under the terms of the 1819 Act. The Magistrates agreed with Mr Hewett:

> *David Royston, Collector of Tolls at St Ives Bridge Bar, was convicted before a full bench of Magistrates in this town, in the penalty of £5 for taking illegal toll on the information of G.G. Hewett, Esq.*

The Bury-Stratton Trust, like many other Turnpike Trusts, 'farmed' out its toll gates. This process, an early form of privatisation, was undertaken every year. The Trust advertised the lowest price it would accept for each gate along its road, and invited bids at auction. A successful bidder took over (or sub-let again) the toll gate and paid the agreed annual rent in monthly instalments to the Clerk of the Trust. Any toll monies collected above the agreed rent were the profit of the gate keeper. This arrangement gave the Trust a guaranteed income and encouraged assiduous collecting of tolls. David Royston had contracted with the Trust for the New Bridge Gate and he employed Staples to live at the Gate and collect the tolls. However as the level of the toll was fixed by the Trust and could not be altered by the gate keeper, Royston's conviction was the responsibility of the Trust.

The law should be obeyed; and the Trust had to consider its position, despite being enraged by the triumph of Mr Hewett. An appeal was lodged, but events in the Assize Court went against the Trust. There was a sorry and unfortunate mess, although it might (just) have been a conspiracy; the convicting Quarter Sessions Magistrate had died in the intervening three months and all the case papers had been mislaid. The appeal could not therefore be heard, with the result that the conviction was upheld. After the lost Appeal the Trust called a meeting for December 7th 1824:

> *for the purpose of taking into consideration the proceedings which have lately been taken and are threatened against David Royston, the Lessee of the Tolls arising at the New Bridge Bar.... and to determine upon the measures to be adopted relative to the same; and if it shall be thought expedient to raise, reduce, or to regulate all or any of the Tolls arising at the said Bar.*

It appears that the Trustees decided to defy the Quarter Sessions ruling. They kept the New Bridge Gate toll at a different rate to that of the other gates – on this matter, the Trust was as resolute as Mr Hewett was stubborn. But Mr Hewett continued his campaign. He found three allies to his cause amongst the Trustees – George Youd, Edward Theed and James Linton, and demanded a special meeting in January 1825. Once again he was unable to secure a majority vote.

Business at the New Bridge Gate

When the toll gates were let for the coming year of 1825 the list advertised the New Bridge Gate at £444 – the highest of the seven gates. Next was the St Ives Green End Gate at £406, but, at that and all the other gates the tolls were twice the rate of those at the New Bridge Gate.

Mr Hewett argued that the Trust must adhere to the legislation of the 1819 Act of Parliament and charge equal tolls at all gates. He disagreed with the forced reduction of the New Bridge toll, because he felt that it was achieved by the votes of those Trustees who were businessmen in St Ives; he alleged that they had fixed a low toll in order to further their vested interests in commercial travel to the town. Mr Hewett tried to rally *every impartial Trustee* to his cause. But by arguing that the New Bridge toll should be the same as all the other tolls, Mr Hewett was actually insisting on a rise in the level of toll at St Ives – and that would have caused even more St Ives Trustees to vote against him.

When the Trust refused to comply with both Court rulings, Mr Hewett became even more determined. Undeterred by cost and the farcical situation of one Trustee seeking a zealous revenge against the whole Trust, he took his case to the High Court. The Trust was first invited to defend its actions; the Trustees had to take into consideration a Ruling of the Court of King's Bench and *shew cause why a writ of Mandamus should not issue directed to them, commanding them to call a Meeting for the purpose of establishing an uniform Rate of Tolls at all the different Toll gates on the line of the said Road.* The case for the defence failed and a High Court Writ of Mandamus was issued against the Trust. St Ives would have talked about nothing else.

The Writ of Mandamus [a legal commandment that a public duty be obeyed]

> *Whereas we have been informed that you the said Trustees have been required to call a meeting for the purpose of establishing an uniform rate of Tolls to be taken at all the different Toll Gates – Yet you well knowing the premises, but not regarding your duty in this behalf, have neglected and refused and still do neglect and refuse to call such a meeting as to make such uniform rate of Tolls in contempt of us and to the great damage of all our liege subjects, Whereupon they have humbly besought us that a fit and speedy recovery may be applied in this respect, And we being willing that due and speedy justice should be done in the premises Do command you that immediately after the receipt of this writ you do call a meeting for the purpose of establishing an uniform rate of Tolls and that you do all acts necessary to be done by you or that you shew us cause to the contrary, And how you shall have executed this our writ make known to us at Westminster on Monday next after the morrow of All Souls, And this you are not to omit on peril that may fall thereon. June 6th 1825*

The Trust called an immediate meeting to hear a first-hand report of the High Court case. Greene and Allpress were the St Ives lawyers who handled the Trust's general affairs and they may have advised on the case, and instructed a barrister to defend the Trust in the High Court. It is expensive to lose a High Court action, and the Trust had incurred legal expenses of over £600 - Mr Hewett's honour proved costly. Despite the public humiliation and financial pain this Writ had to be obeyed; the Trust had five months by which time it had to present a scheme of uniform tolls to the High Court. The Clerk called a meeting, but this meeting did not sort out the problem, nor did a further four meetings on July 16th, 26th and 30th and August 16th 1825. The Trustees could not agree the best way forward. If they set an unpopular toll rate they risked further antagonism and humiliation if it was forced down, but sufficient money still had to be raised to pay off the debts for both the building of the New Bridges and the newly incurred legal fees. The Trust was faced with a very difficult dilemma but it needed to retain its authority and hence its notices remained ebullient.

Fig. 24 View of Bridge Street and 'The Crown Inn', c.1940
The majority of the Bury-Stratton Trustee meetings were held in 'The Crown Inn' (at the top, centre of the photo). 'The Crown Inn' was demolished in June 1975 after a fire. Woolworths now occupy the replacement building.
Norris Museum PH/S.IVE/Bdge.St/24

Fig. 25 The New Bridges and cattle grazing in Wilhorn Meadow

St Ives and Politics and Money

The arguments over the New Bridges toll were extensive, persistent and bitter. They were not only about administrative policy within the Trust, nor were they dependant upon personalities and the inevitable diversity amongst 178 Trustees. These arguments reflected a serious power struggle in local politics, amidst the background of the growing changes in national politics. And in addition, and by no means least, the arguments were about money and business.

In early 19th century England and Wales, many factors contributed to a call for electoral and political reform, notably, rapid economic development and expansion of population, migration to urban industrial settlements (the big cities), and the frequent agricultural depressions causing rural poverty. An increase in mobility gave broader horizons and ambitions to the population making them less tolerant of local aristocratic power.

This emergence of 'liberalism' was happening in Huntingdonshire and one of its leaders was Samuel Wells. He was a Huntingdon attorney and also one of the Turnpike Trustees. With passionate speeches and rallying political pamphlets, he urged 'independence' from the Tory party and its controlling aristocracy. Wells' inspirational campaign centred on the economic depression and the mood of discontent in the county. He and his party were championed by "The Independent Press". Electioneering on June 17th 1818 he addressed *The Independent Freeholders of the County of Huntingdon:*

> *The maintenance of independence; let us prove to the world that there still exists among the yeomanry of the County the famed spirit of our forefathers. Who is there amongst us*

that does not feel the oppression of the taxes, and the misery of the poor-rates, that does not shudder at the increase of crime, and the maintenance of a standing army in the time of profound peace? Who is there amongst us, however respectable, that does not daily behold some relative or friend verging into pauperism, or actually becoming the inmate of that workhouse many would a short time since have shuddered even to inspect? Taxation, grinding, ruthless taxation, has occasioned these miseries.

Although the Whig candidate did not win a Huntingdonshire seat in the 1818 election, he dramatically upset the accustomed pattern of Tory voting; the cause of the Independents and Whigs gathered momentum in the coming years. A growing middle class of professionals, town businessmen, independent farmers, and an important minority of gentlemen began to assert their voice in the County. They supported Lord John Russell who was elected, unopposed, to one of the two County Parliamentary seats in 1820.

Within Huntingdonshire the reform movement was centred upon St Ives and the Fen villages of Bluntisham, Colne, Earith, Pidley and Somersham; here, as nationally, there was strong support from the large communities of Nonconformists or Dissenters. St Ives strained against the yoke of two masters. The first was their absentee 'landlord' – the Duke of Manchester - who was Governor of Jamaica. And the second was Huntingdon, which, despite being smaller than St Ives, was the County town holding all the administrative and legal power and two Borough Parliamentary seats. In the 1826 Parliamentary election the Whigs sought to rally support in St Ives:

> *To the honour of the old town, and its unshackled, free and enlightened Freeholders, the inhabitants of St Ives have stood forward and by their noble conduct they have declared that they will not have their representatives previously nominated by a combination of powerful interests.*

But *the powerful interests,* in particular the Montagu families of the Duke of Manchester and the Earl of Sandwich, poured enormous amounts of money into their campaign to oust Lord John Russell and ensure that the County returned to their Tory control. The Tory costs were £13,384-7s-3d for an electorate of 1744 freeholders - about £7-15s per man. Apart from £1558 declared as *Bills paid for Favours,* the majority of expenses were £6834 for *Inkeepers Bills thro' the County.* The election took place in Huntingdon and lasted five days, during which time the candidates provided, as was customary, accommodation and generous hospitality for their voters; in a very tight contest the Tories managed to secure the necessary votes for success.

The Poll Books for the 1818 and 1826 Parliamentary elections show which Trustees voted for the Whig candidate. There were the St Ives businessmen – for example, Thomas Hutchinson a currier, Edward Jennings a mill owner, John Johnson a grocer, John Ashton a corn merchant. There were the land owners - Robert and Richard Daintree and John Bonfoy Rooper. Other Trustees who were St Ives businessmen but who were not freeholders and therefore did not have a vote, were active members of the nonconformist chapels and can be assumed to be largely Whig supporters - John Franks a tailor, Robert Knightley a shoemaker, and Thomas Ulph an ironmonger who spoke at the dinner for Russell after the 1826 election. The Trust was supported by another St Ives Whig who was not (at that time) a Trustee but who was certainly very influential and passionately committed to working towards reform and improvement in St Ives - this was George Game Day. In contrast, Mr Hewett was a Tory voter and a member of the established Church of England.

Politics in the Trust

Unfortunately no records remain to show which Trustees voted, and moreover how they voted, at the numerous Turnpike Trust meetings concerning the New Bridges. The majority of meetings were held in the Crown Inn, St Ives, almost within sight of the New Bridges. Of those Trustees who have been traced, at least 44 either lived in St Ives or owned businesses there. These men could have dominated the meetings; it was easy for them to attend and they would have been keen to be closely involved in decisions which directly affected their livelihood. Other Trustees, such as Godfrey Thornton who held land at Hemingford Abbots but lived in London, and John Carstairs who had land at Warboys but lived in Essex, probably attended fewer meetings and were more remote from the day to day running of the Trust.

Mr Hewett resented the St Ives Trustees, comparing them to pirates and bandits. He felt they were usurpers acting against the interests of the Trust and the road as a whole. Although Mr Hewett finally 'nailed' the St Ives Trustees on a point of law over the unequal tolls, he had probably always opposed the building of the New Bridges by the Trust. In his letters he had argued that the New Bridges did not benefit the Warboys or Gamlingay farmers, whereas they did benefit the St Ives businessmen, and that it therefore should be the St Ives businessmen who should pay – not the rest of the Bury-Stratton road.

There was some truth in Mr Hewett's argument. The New Bridges were built because the St Ives businessmen were not prepared to wait for the Duke of Manchester. For the first time in the town's existence there was an alternative body to the controlling Lord of the Manor (Ramsey Abbey, the Crown or the Dukes of Manchester) which was sufficiently powerful to effect major changes in St Ives. This was the Turnpike Trust. The businessmen of St Ives had grasped their opportunity, and with the financial support of John Margetts, they had used the Trust to the best advantage of their town.

During the time of planning and building the New Bridges, the economic climate in Huntingdonshire, an agricultural county, had grown steadily worse. Enclosure had made the farm labourers dependant upon the farmers, but the farmers could not afford to pay wages throughout the year, and as a result the 'Poor Rate' increased by 25% between 1800 and 1813. The situation was exacerbated by widespread unemployment with the return of soldiers and sailors at the end of the Napoleonic Wars, and the use of cheap, itinerant Irish labour. Falling grain prices had been artificially held up by the passing of the Corn Laws to restrict cheap imports, but a series of poor harvests compounded the agricultural depressions. National taxes remained high to pay the debt of war. At the very worst level the poor could choose, either to suffer starvation or risk draconian punishments for poaching. County meetings were held, and petitions for agricultural relief were made to parliament; when none came social unrest flared, and was severely repressed – five men were hanged and many transported after riots in Littleport, near Ely in 1816.

The St Ives Trustees were caught in a desperate situation. They had built the New Bridges at a cost of nearly £400,000 in today's money, and they could only pay this debt by the collection of tolls. These businessmen were acutely sensitive to the impact of any rise in toll rates, and knew they could not charge the full toll at the New Bridges – it would cripple the town.

The High Court, Mr Hewett and the Duke offered no sympathy to St Ives' economic problems.

A truce is agreed

Meanwhile, the legality of the Trust had to be restored. Five men called a special meeting; William Wiles, the Reverend Thomas Johnston, George Thomson, George Ekins, John Longland and Edward Theed. The meeting's agenda offered a wide variety of options in the search for a compromise so that a solution to the toll problem might finally be agreed: *A meeting to take into consideration the propriety of discontinuing, altering or removing the situation of the Wareseley and Potton Toll gates, the New Bridge Toll gate, and also the St Ives Green End Toll gate, all, any or either of them.*

"The Independent Press" had judiciously maintained a silence during the issuing of the Writ, but it reported in full on the meeting of August 16th 1825. Although the report was clearly supportive of the Trust, it was dignified, and was designed to mark the end of the whole affair; as such, it must have been appreciated by the Trust.

> *On Tuesday a numerous meeting of the Trustees of the Bury and Stratton Road was held at the Crown Inn, St Ives.*
> *Mr Allpress read over the consents of five-sixths of the creditors for the reduction of the tolls, but stated that the requisite number of consents had not been given for the removal of any of the gates. It will be in the recollection of our readers, that about three years ago, a line of arches was erected over the low ground on the Fenstanton side of the old bridge, to guard against the too frequent accidents occasioned by inundations: and in order that the entire line of road should not be taxed for this particular work, a separate toll of three half-pence was collected; but a mandamus was procured at the instance of Mr Hewett, of*

Hilton, from the Court of King's Bench, commanding the Trustees to make an even rate of toll along the whole line of road, in conformity with the Act of Parliament. At a late meeting, the tolls were all regulated to the highest rate.

It was ultimately agreed that all the toll gates should remain, but that the rate of toll should be equally reduced.   *Vide Advertisement.*

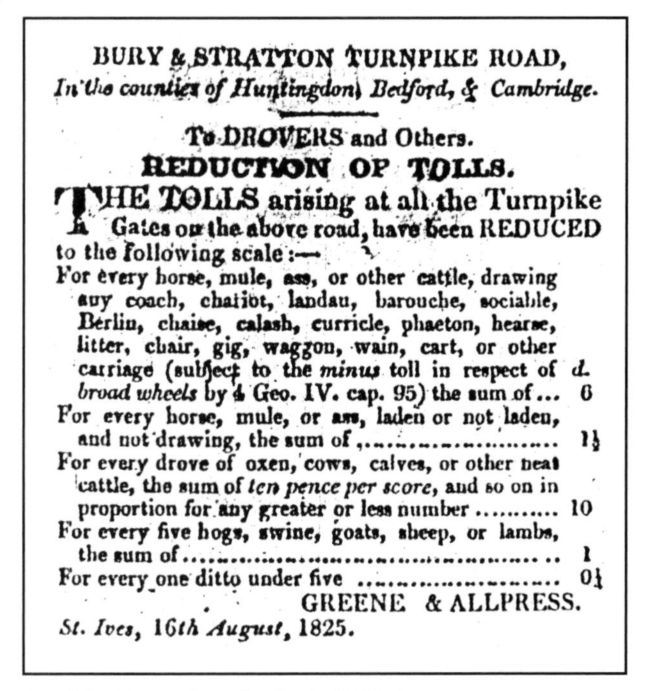

BURY & STRATTON TURNPIKE ROAD,

In the counties of Huntingdon, Bedford, & Cambridge.

To DROVERS and Others.

REDUCTION OF TOLLS.

THE TOLLS arising at all the Turnpike Gates on the above road, have been REDUCED to the following scale:—

	d.
For every horse, mule, ass, or other cattle, drawing any coach, chariot, landau, barouche, sociable, Berlin, chaise, calash, curricle, phaeton, hearse, litter, chair, gig, waggon, wain, cart, or other carriage (subject to the *minus* toll in respect of *broad wheels* by 4 Geo. IV. cap. 95) the sum of...	6
For every horse, mule, or ass, laden or not laden, and not drawing, the sum of	1½
For every drove of oxen, cows, calves, or other neat cattle, the sum of *ten pence per score*, and so on in proportion for any greater or less number	10
For every five hogs, swine, goats, sheep, or lambs, the sum of..	1
For every one ditto under five	0¼

GREENE & ALLPRESS.

St. Ives, 16*th August*, 1825.

Fig. 26 Poster for reduction in Toll Prices
The Huntingdon, Bedford and Peterborough Gazette, & Independent Press, August 20th 1825

Fig. 27 Milestones of the Bury-Stratton road
Milestones were compulsory on all turnpiked roads from 1767. Many milestones have since disappeared. During the Second World War milestones were removed, hidden or deliberately defaced to thwart German invaders; subsequently many were never reinstated. Others have been lost to road-widening schemes, or damaged by vehicle accidents or grass verge cutters. In 2001 the Milestone Society was established, and has worked extensively "to identify, record, research and conserve the milestones of the British Isles". See also maps on pages 26-27.

Thomas Telford visits St Ives and admires the New Bridges

About a year after the litigation had been resolved and the destructive arguments over tolls exhausted, Thomas Telford came to St Ives in 1826 and saw the New Bridges.

Telford was the most famous civil engineer of the late 18th and early 19th century – his friend, the poet Robert Southey, nicknamed him *The Colossus of Roads.* For over 50 years the scope and scale of his work was prodigious; notably, a large series of roads, bridges and harbours in the Scottish Highlands, the Caledonian Canal in Scotland, the Gotha Canal in Sweden, and the London to Holyhead road with the suspension bridge over the Menai Straits. In East Anglia he worked on various Fen drainage and engineering projects, and the infamous Eau Brink Cut. (The bitter political infighting over this work to divert the River Great Ouse from a long bend in its course near Kings Lynn lasted over 30 years; there were three full years of 'debate' in Parliament, one for each mile of cut. Telford, a supremely practical man, was said to have found this experience unpleasant and frustrating, and as a result did not enjoy working in the Fens.)

The Commissioners of Navigation of the Great Ouse had asked Telford to investigate the river between St Ives staunch and Earith. His concluding report was delivered to the Quarterly Meeting of the Commissioners at the Crown Inn, Kings Lynn on October 12th 1826; he recommended major dredging works, a new side cut, a new staunch and 'stop gates' at an estimated cost of over £4000.

Telford, or perhaps one of his assistants, made six drawings of the Ouse, of which three have survived; one of these is the "Plan and Elevation of the Bridge and Causeway at St Ives". This fine drawing of the bridges and, in particular, the detailed measurement of all 55 arches of the New Bridges, seems to be largely outside his remit from the Commissioners. The drawing is in ink and watercolour with a careful use of shading. However there are some inconsistencies, particularly in the elevation of St Ives Bridge where, for example, details of the chapel are inaccurate and look more like a sketch than an architect's drawing. The New Bridges elevation has the string course in the wrong place, and the cross section omits the taper in the parapet. But it is interesting that the New Bridges drawing has a cross section which contains the measurements of the underground wooden pegs securing the edges of the brick floor inverts. To draw this, Telford may have been shown one of the construction drawings or may have talked to someone involved in its building, or his vast experience as a bridge builder might have enabled him to 'assess' the probable length of the pegs from standard practice. But we can be sure that details such as the length of the pegs were irrelevant to the river navigation - it would appear that Telford admired the newly built causeway, and, apart from drawing it for his own personal interest, he may have been making a record of the structure for the new reference library at the Institute of Civil Engineers. When he became the first President of the ICE in 1821 he wrote to his friends and fellow engineers:

> *You will remind them to send me drawings and descriptions of works really executed. We have no wish for learned discussions. Facts and practical operations are to compose our collections. Perseverance will in time render the collection of Books, Manuscripts and Drawings invaluable.*

Telford would have noted that the newly built New Bridges were neither innovative in design nor construction, but he would have recognised that the 55 brick arches were, at that time, exceptional. In the coming Industrial Age brick bridges with multiple arches would be built in great numbers and to great heights and lengths; that would be when the railways would demand enormous viaducts to provide suitable track gradients for the locomotives and, at the same time, facilitate the transport of bricks.

The Bury-Stratton Trust, with the Duke of Manchester's agreement, had not had any visions of pioneering architecture; they had copied a standard pattern for a vehicular causeway – a road on arches, or viaduct. They had agreed on this simple, functional structure, which was determined by local circumstances - the topography of the flood plain, the availability of river-borne bricks, and cost. But they had built a unique bridge; in 1822 the New Bridges were the longest road causeway with the greatest number of continuous brick arches.

Fig 28 The upstream side of the New Bridges viewed from the Hemingford Meadow: 55 arches stretching over 220 yards

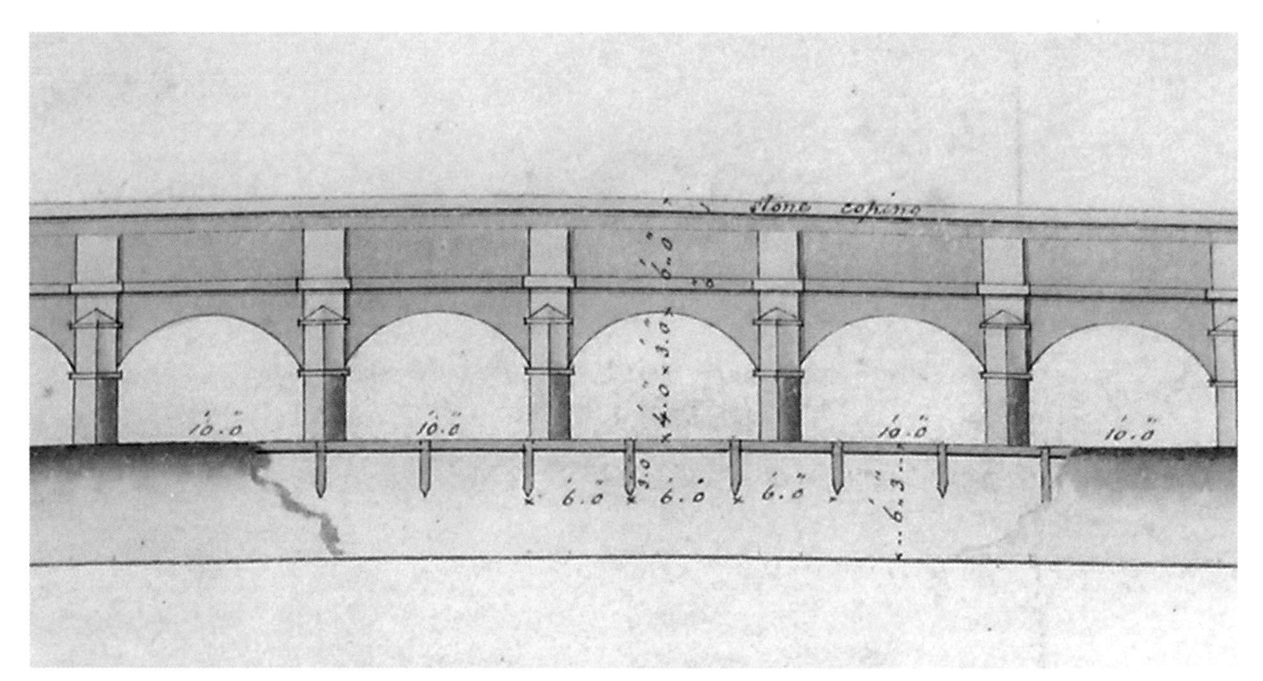

Fig. 29 Thomas Telford's drawing of the causeway.
The elevation drawing shows the west (upstream) side of the New Bridges. Despite its detailed drawing and measurements, it is slightly inaccurate: the buttresses are shown with a string course running across them and triangular caps above it – but in fact the string course is above the triangular caps which are level with the springing of the arches. There are two possible explanations. Either Telford's draughtsman was copying the original design for the causeway which the builders did not strictly adhere to, or Telford's draughtsman misinterpreted his notes when he got back to the office to make the final drawing; the first is the more likely.

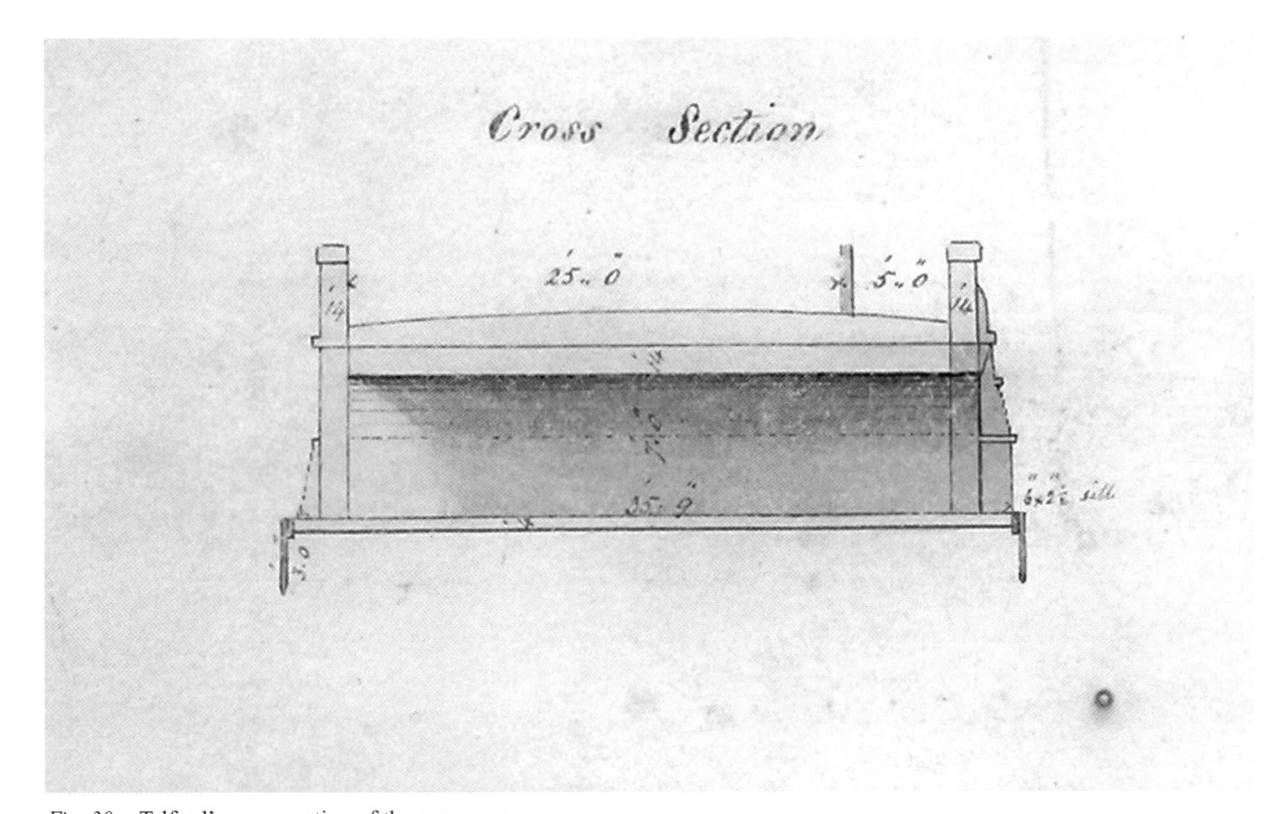

Fig. 30 Telford's cross-section of the causeway
This drawing contains another interesting detail suggesting that Telford may have had access to the original construction design for the New Bridges, or that he talked to someone involved in its building. Telford records the length of the wooden pegs which supported the brick paved inverts of the arches. The drawing cannot have been made any earlier than its date of 1826 because the watermark on the paper is 'Wattman, 1826', and by that time the pegs were buried in the ground.

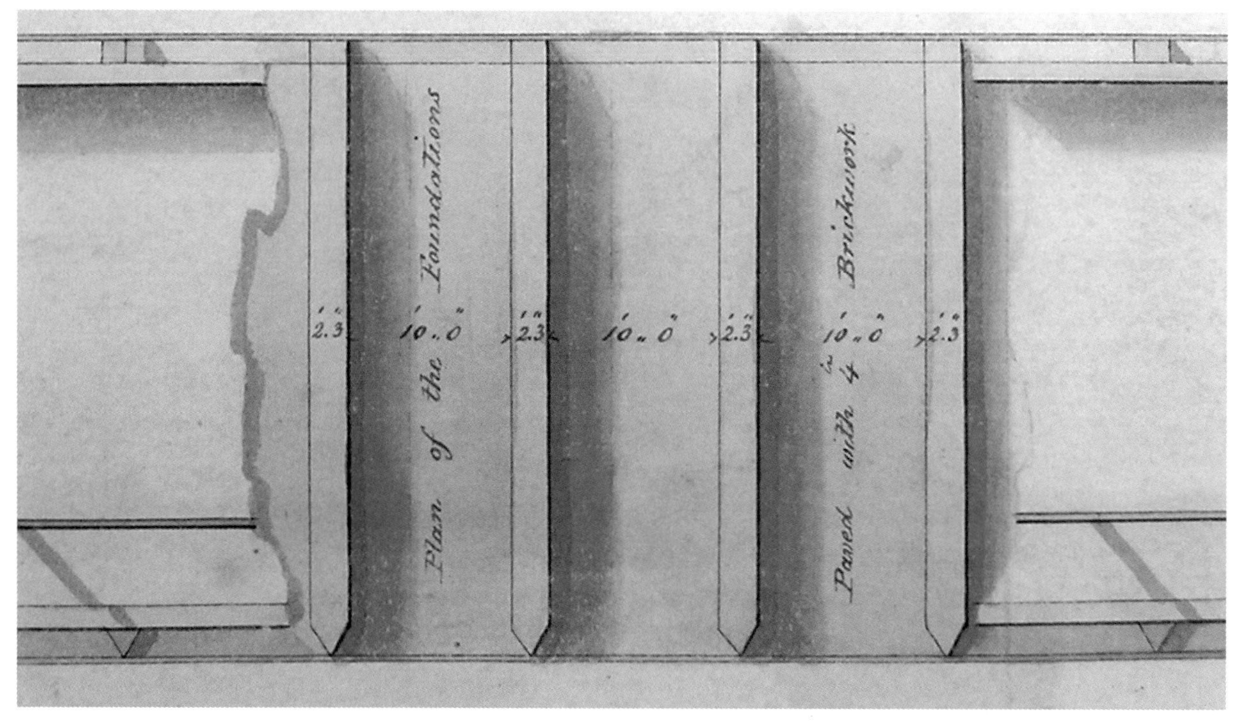

Fig. 31 Telford's drawing of the foundations

The drawing shows the road as it was in its early days with a five foot-wide path for pedestrians on the west side. It was marked from the roadway with a set of wooden railings. The scale of the drawing is: five eighths of an inch = 10 feet, i.e. 'a sixteenth inch scale': one sixteenth of an inch = 1 foot.

Telford's drawing of 'The Bridge and Causeway at St Ives' is owned by St Ives Town Council

Ten years later

The New Bridge Gate was the busiest of the Bury-Stratton Trust's seven gates; it generated nearly a third of the income from the whole road. Between 1826 and 1833 the New Bridge Gate earned about £80 per month, the next highest being the St Ives Green End Gate with £35. In March 1833 the Trust decided to remove the New Bridge toll gate because its receipts of over £6000 had paid off all the debts incurred in the building of the New Bridges. "The Independent Press" editorial agreed with the Trust:

> *The toll was very proper until the new bridge was paid for, from its collection beyond that, its continuance was both unjust and oppressive.*

But the rest of the editorial conveyed harsh criticism of the Bury-Stratton Trust and its road. Attitudes had changed considerably in the 11 years since the building of the New Bridges:

> *The Trustees, of a comparatively insignificant by-road from an obscure village in Huntingdonshire, to a place equally obscure in Bedfordshire, [have] contrived to tax all people travelling on their road passing through the town, even but a few yards, with a toll both in and out. Perhaps no town in England has suffered more injustice by the infliction of tolls than St Ives.*

Unfortunately for the Trust, Mr Hewett did not agree with the removal of the New Bridges toll, and once again he stoked an enormous public row. Mr Hewett gathered around him a very small group of like-minded Trustees and together they launched a continuous and bitter assault for nine months. With some prescience rather than coincidence, the editor of "The Independent Press" announced in March 1833 that forthwith all correspondents *must furnish us with their names.* The editor then allowed space in his newspaper for the battle; twelve letters and five editorials were printed about the New Bridge Gate. At its best this made for public debate and public inquiry, and at its worst, defamation of character and near libel.

Mr Hewett said that, yet again, the St Ives Trustees were acting only in their own interests. In order to be fair to travellers along the whole length of road, he argued, the New Bridge Gate should remain and there should be a uniform reduction in tolls at all the gates. Mr Hewett found no support; it seemed that everybody else wanted the New Bridge Gate removed as soon as possible. Market traders and drovers doing business in St Ives wanted to pay one less toll. The Hemingford and Fenstanton villagers and St Ives townspeople particularly wanted the New Bridge Gate removed, because unlike the Duke of Manchester's Bridge toll, it offered them no exemption from payment. After ten years of paying tolls to go both in and out of the town everyone (except Mr Hewett) felt they had well and truly paid for the New Bridges.

Mr Hewett persisted and threatened further litigation. He called meeting after meeting of the Trustees, whilst his letters to the newspaper became increasingly vituperative. At last, under the respected leadership of the St Ives solicitor, George Game Day and Matthew Tebbutt, a prominent St Ives Whig, Mr Hewett was finally defeated on November 22nd 1833 when a Trust meeting decided:

> *by a most impeccable and overwhelming majority, that the tolls at the gate should cease, the gate be removed, and the toll house be taken down and the materials sold.*

The Trust was rid of its oppressor and St Ives was freed from a toll gate. News spread rapidly:

> *A great concourse of the inhabitants of St Ives assembled to witness the ceremony of pulling down the New Bridge Gate, and at twelve o'clock precisely the gate was taken off its hinges amidst the shouts and acclamations of the populace. The church bells were ringing merrily, and the St Ives band attended to enliven the workmen employed in removing the gate, root and branch. In the evening there was a brilliant display of fire-works in honour of the event, in the Sheep Market, prepared and arranged by the celebrated pyrotechnist, Mr Gyngell.*

A defeated Mr Hewett saw the events in a different light and roundly criticised the newspaper report as scurrilous. He felt he had been grossly insulted by:

> *a mob, collected by a band of music, to whom beer had been given.*

Both accounts of the taking down of the New Bridge Gate agree that it was a highly charged affair, with the crowd eager to celebrate their freedom from a tax. This demonstration by ordinary townsfolk against a turnpike toll gate was not dissimilar to the infamous 'Rebecca riots' in South Wales in 1839. There rioters disguised themselves in women's clothing as 'Rebecca and her daughters', and smashed down turnpike gates. The immediate cause of grievance was the burden of the tolls, but this was exacerbated by rural poverty, an increase in tithe payments and the new Union Workhouse system. The nonconformist rioters took their identity from a biblical text:

And they blessed Rebekah and said unto her..... 'Let thy seed possess the gates of those which hate them'. (Genesis 24: v 60)

Mr Hewett, it seems, was completely out of touch with popular feeling and the state of the county around him. Agriculture was even more depressed than ten years previously. There were riots in St Ives in 1831 over the use of Irish labour. The 'Captain Swing' riots in 1830 and 1831 protested against the introduction of threshing machines; these riots were widespread across southern England, and in Huntingdonshire occurred in Upton, Hamerton, Buckworth, Old Weston and Sawtry. Parliamentary Commissioners reported from Huntingdonshire:

farmers so burdened with rent, tithes, taxes for the poor and church rate, that they could not employ or pay labour.

No one was in any mood to listen to Mr Hewett. He and his group persisted in calling further meetings to reinstate the New Bridge toll gate but they *were negatived by an immense majority*. Mr Hewett died a few months later on June 12th 1834 in Enfield, Middlesex. The brief notice in "The Cambridge Chronicle" said:

he will be long remembered in the parish in which he resided.

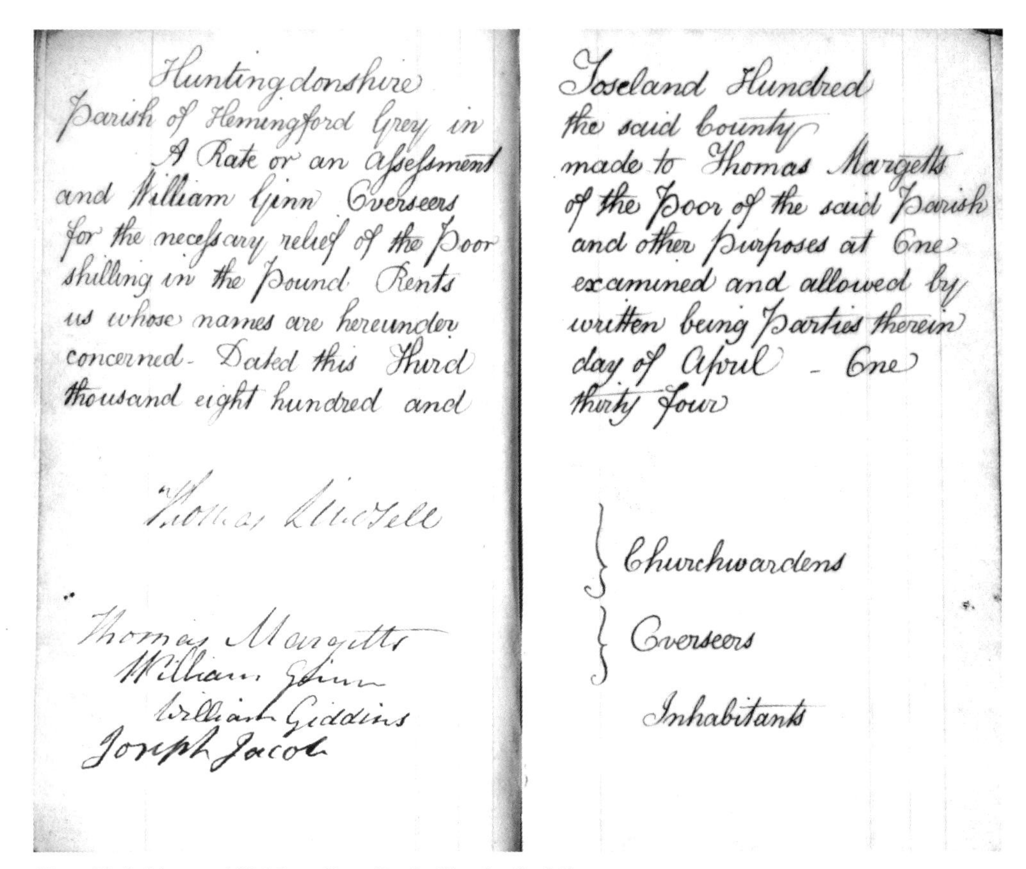

Huntingdonshire Toseland Hundred
Parish of Hemingford Grey in the said County
A Rate or an Assessment made to Thomas Margetts
and William Ginn Overseers of the Poor of the said Parish
for the necessary relief of the Poor and other Purposes at One
shilling in the Pound Rents examined and allowed by
us whose names are hereunder written being Parties therein
concerned - Dated this Third day of April - One
thousand eight hundred and thirty four

Thomas [illegible] } Churchwardens

Thomas Margetts
William Ginn } Overseers

William Giddins
Joseph Jacob Inhabitants

Figs. 32 & 33 1834 Poor Rate Book, Hemingford Grey
The tax levied for the Poor Rate was one shilling in the pound on assessed property values. This ledger shows the details of the property acreage, its situation, occupier, owner and rateable value. It is a comprehensive survey of the Parish of Hemingford Grey.

Occupiers	A	R	P	£	s	d	Proprietors	£	s	d
Middleton Mrs Guest marsh &c	61	3	15	80	7	7	Bishop of Ely			
Cow close &c	19	2	-	23	8	0	"			
	13	1	20	22	1	7	Thornhill			
Meadow	7	3	8	11	14	-	"			
Homestead &c	8	2	32	14	15	9	"			
	5	1	7	5	5	11	"			
Tansey Close &c	3	3	32	6	18	3	"			
long lane Do	2	3	14	4	18	11	"			
	7	1	19	3	2	9	"			
				172	12	9		X 8	12	8
Nicholls W. Meadow	1	2	5	2	6		Nicholls			
" Mill Field	5	1	9	9	5	10	"			
Gore close	6	2	34	10	1	4	Warner			
Homestead &c	1		22	1	2	9	Nicholls	X 1	2	9
				22	15	11		9	15	5

St Ivians may have freed themselves from one toll – but they were to see it immediately replaced by another. In accordance with the original agreement, when the Bury-Stratton Trust had paid all the building costs, the New Bridges were to be handed over to the Duke who would then recommence his St Ives Bridge toll.

And no sooner had the Trust freed itself from Mr Hewett than it was attacked on another front by an equally litigious but much more powerful adversary – the Duke of Manchester. The Duke said he was not prepared to accept the New Bridges if that meant accepting the responsibility of their future repair. He ignored criticism that he was reneging on his deal with the Trustees, and proceeded to take legal advice as to whether he could successfully challenge the agreement. In a statement to the Solicitor General he explained his concerns, complained about the condition of the New Bridges, and said that he was quite prepared to pull down the New Bridges to avoid any encumbrance of expense. The Solicitor General sternly rebutted his claims:

> *He cannot contend that he is to receive his Tolls and to do no repairs. His obligation to repair attaches upon the new Works. I apprehend that his Grace could not now fill up the Arches and reduce the Road to the condition in which it was before the Act. The Trustees are bound to put the whole in perfect repair but if they do so I would advise His Grace not to further contest the matter with them. December 1833*

The Duke had complained that the New Bridges side walls were: *out of their perpendicular and want repairing and the Arches pointing.* His arguments continued into the next year until the Trust organised and paid for the necessary repairs. 90 feet of wall were rebuilt. Two entries in the Accounts ledger in December 1834 detail: *Mr J. Sutton, by order of William Biggs: £6-2s-6d and Messrs Everett & Wakefield, by order of William Biggs: £32-10s-0d.*

After that the New Bridges were given up by the Trust and transferred to the Duke of Manchester.

Fig 34 A view through an arch of the New Bridges
The level of the meadow has risen with the accumulation of flood silt deposits over many years since the arches were built; this now restricts the flow of flood water through the arches.
Photo courtesy of The Cambridge Evening News

Fig. 35 St Ives. Lithograph by J. Hunter, mid 19th century
The New Bridges can be seen in the top right of this picture. St Ives is shown in a scene of contented prosperity. The view of the town begins with the Parish Church; the Christianity of St Ives is shown in the established Church of England. (It is probable that the many Dissenters in St Ives would have seen the town differently). Smoking chimneys in the town and gangs of lighters on the river depict commerce. Plentiful stocks of grazing sheep and cattle show the extent of the town's livestock trade. Well dressed citizens stroll at leisure and enjoy a boat trip on the river.
Norris Museum, St Ives *PWD/S.IVE/38*

TO THE MEMORY OF JOHN MARGETTS
HIGH SHERIFF OF CAMBS AND HUNTS IN 1827.
WHO DIED AT WISTOW IN 1842, AGED 77.
AND WAS ENTOMBED BENEATH THIS CHURCH:
ALSO TO HIS YOUNGER BROTHER WILLIAM,
WHO DIED S.P. IN 1818. THE ONLY SONS OF
Jn MARGETTS OF HEMINGFORD GREY,
AND OF MARY HIS WIFE,
ELDEST DAUGHTER OF
ROWLAND RUGELEY OF POTTON

Fig. 36 John Margetts' memorial in St Ives Parish Church

John Margetts and his brother William are remembered on a modest brass plaque, sited high up at the end of the south aisle. This is in marked contrast to the ornate and significant stone memorials of other St Ivians along the same aisle, and also to the Margetts' family memorials in Hemingford Grey Church. William Margetts had no children, and John Margetts' children took the name of their mother's lawful husband. So it is probable that this memorial was erected by John Margetts' cousins or nephews; they made particular mention of his office as High Sheriff of Cambridgeshire and Huntingdonshire – an honour for the Margetts family name. John Margetts must have been a man of strong personality; although he was a very prosperous businessman from an influential Tory family and was appointed High Sheriff, his personal circumstances of marrying an un-divorced woman at Gretna Green were, to say the least, unconventional.

Perhaps John Margetts is better remembered in the New Bridges; he certainly was the force that cut through the arguments and got the New Bridges built.

The coming of the Railway and the end of the Turnpike

In 1824 and 1825 there was much talk of a new system of transport - the railway. The Northern Railway Company had been set up in 1824 with a rush of investors eager to profit from the venture. The railway's route from London to York was planned to go through Cambridge and Huntingdon. "The Independent Press" entertained its readers with this novelty:

> *30th April 1825: Several persons have been employed during the present week surveying the neighbourhood of this town to ascertain the practicability of constructing the new Northern Rail-road, which it is now said, will certainly take its course thro' this part of the country. After leaving Cambridge, it will proceed over Godmanchester Common, (by a bridge of boats, we presume); it will then extend across the river, (leaving Huntingdon to the left, as a place incorrigible of improvement) by an aerial chain suspension bridge; through Hartford (over the church) from whence it will take a Northerly direction in a straight line – to the moon!*

Such frivolity did not last long. On September 27th 1825 the Stockton to Darlington railway was opened and in 1829 Stephenson's engine 'Rocket' reached a previously undreamed-of speed of almost 30 miles per hour. Stage coaches could not compete - their top speeds, when travelling, were 10 miles per hour. The 1821 advertisement for the Day Coach via St Ives had offered: *Expeditious travelling. From Wisbech to London in Eleven Hours!*

The opportunities that the railway offered to a town's business and prosperity seemed limitless. In May 1834 a meeting was held: *at the request of upwards of 50 of the influential gentlemen of Huntingdon and St Ives,* and a committee was formed to encourage the rail companies to build a line to St Ives. This committee was led by George Game Day and about half of its members were also trustees of the Bury-Stratton road.

The St Ives to Godmanchester railway crosses the New Bridges

Exactly 25 years after the New Bridges were built the railways arrived at St Ives and the town was wildly enthusiastic when two railway lines opened on the same day – 17th August 1847. The Eastern Counties Railway had brought a line from Chesterton Junction, Cambridge to St Ives, and the Ely and Huntingdon Railway constructed a line from St Ives to Godmanchester.

The section of railway from St Ives to Godmanchester was expensive; four and three-quarter miles had cost over £120,000 to build, largely due to the number of bridges. There were four crossings of the Great Ouse River channels with heavy wooden viaducts, and at St Ives the railway was carried above the flood meadows on long wooden trestle-bridge causeways to cross over the top of the New Bridges. A gated level-crossing was built on the roadway of the New Bridges and the four arches below had to be strengthened with heavier brickwork to take the weight of the trains.

Unfortunately revenues on the St Ives to Godmanchester line did not match expectations. Although the service had begun with six daily trains, it soon dwindled to one, and on October 1st 1849 the financial situation was so bad that all trains had to be stopped. For three months the only service to be seen on the rail tracks over the New Bridges was a horse-drawn tram seating 60 passengers. This contravened the Railway Act of 1844 which required companies to provide a minimum travelling speed of 12 mph for passenger trains; the Railway Commissioners could empower the closure of the line or the Company's lease. Some freight operations and two daily passenger services were re-introduced from January 1st 1850, but there was little improvement until rail links with Huntingdon were built – transfers by road carriage from Godmanchester to Huntingdon were inherently unsatisfactory. Services improved when cross-country links opened to Kettering in 1866 and to March, Lincoln and Doncaster in 1883.

By the 1850s when a countrywide network of railways was established, the stage coaches inevitably ceased, and this hastened the end of the turnpike trusts. Local roads had seen an increase in traffic as they acted as 'feeders' to the railway stations, but on the main roads, the turnpike trusts saw a significant decline in their revenues and many became bankrupt. As a result the trusts were dissolved - abandoning the repair of their roads to the parishes until the Highway Act of 1862 compelled parishes to unite under Highway Boards. In 1878 the Quarter Sessions took on some of the costs, and in 1888 the new County Councils took over responsibility for main roads. Local roads were to be managed by Urban and District Councils.

St Ives receives the Telford drawing

In 1905 the New Bridges were unexpectedly thrust again into the limelight. The trustees of the estate of Thomas Telford were rationalising his papers to create a national archive. His drawing of St Ives Bridge and the New Bridges was deemed surplus to requirements, and was sent as a gift to St Ives Town Council

– in Cornwall, from whence it was forwarded to St Ives in Huntingdonshire. A letter from Mr Elliott Odams to "The Hunts Post" newspaper describes the civic pride felt in St Ives on receipt of Telford's plan:

> *'Lyndhurst', St Ives. May 15th 1905*
> *Sir, The receipt of the great engineer's plan and elevation of the bridge – the old and new bridges and Causeway – is opportune. The plan is architecturally a grand work of engineering skill; I am glad to know that it is the intention of the St Ives Town Council to have the plan framed and hung up in their Chamber. In doing so they will, in my opinion, be honouring themselves, the town and the memory of the great and good Scotchman.*

At that time Town Council meetings took place in the Corn Exchange or in the solicitors' offices of the Day family, of whom successive generations were Town Clerks. And so the drawing was hung in Mr George Dennis Day's office, now Leeds Day solicitors in the Broadway, to remain there until 2003.

Fig 37 The stamp on the reverse of the drawing of 'The Bridge and Causeway at St Ives'
In 2004 the drawing was professionally restored and a facsimile made. The facsimile will hang in the St Ives Town Council Chamber and the original will return to Leeds Day's offices where the restricted daylight will continue to preserve its fragile watercolours.

The Duke of Manchester relinquishes the New Bridges

The maintenance and ownership of the New Bridges remained with the Duchy of Manchester. In 1918 the Ninth Duke's fortunes ran out. He was declared bankrupt and over 5000 acres of his Huntingdonshire estates were sold that year. But the New Bridges, St Ives Bridge and its tolls, and St Ives market tolls were not sold. It would appear that the bridges were an unattractive purchase because their ownership included the liability for repair, but whereas the market and bridge tolls were saleable they were offered in a package with the bridges. Mr Dilley, a local auctioneer, was interested in acquiring the market tolls, as were St Ives Town Council who, in the words of the Mayor: *wished to be masters in their own house.*

Negotiations with the Duke began. The Duchy solicitors introduced a complicated proposal where the bridges would be sold in a three-way deal. If the Huntingdonshire County Council agreed to take the bridges with a single grant of £2000 towards their repair, the Duke would then admit liability to their repair. (He obviously did not want to be made to repair the bridges before the County Council took them over.) St Ives Town Council would make a grant of £500 to the County Council towards the bridges, whilst paying £700 for the market and bridge tolls. The Duke threatened that if this deal was not achieved, he would apply to Parliament for an amendment to the Charter and raise all the tolls. Despite the County Council pointing out that expenditure on the bridges might be nearer £2000 a year rather than a single capital payment of £2000, and the hollowness of the Duke's threat when it was known that the bridge tolls had fallen into abeyance over ten years ago, the deal was signed. The Manchester ownership of St Ives Bridge, causeway and tolls was ended, after almost three hundred years; 1628 -1921.

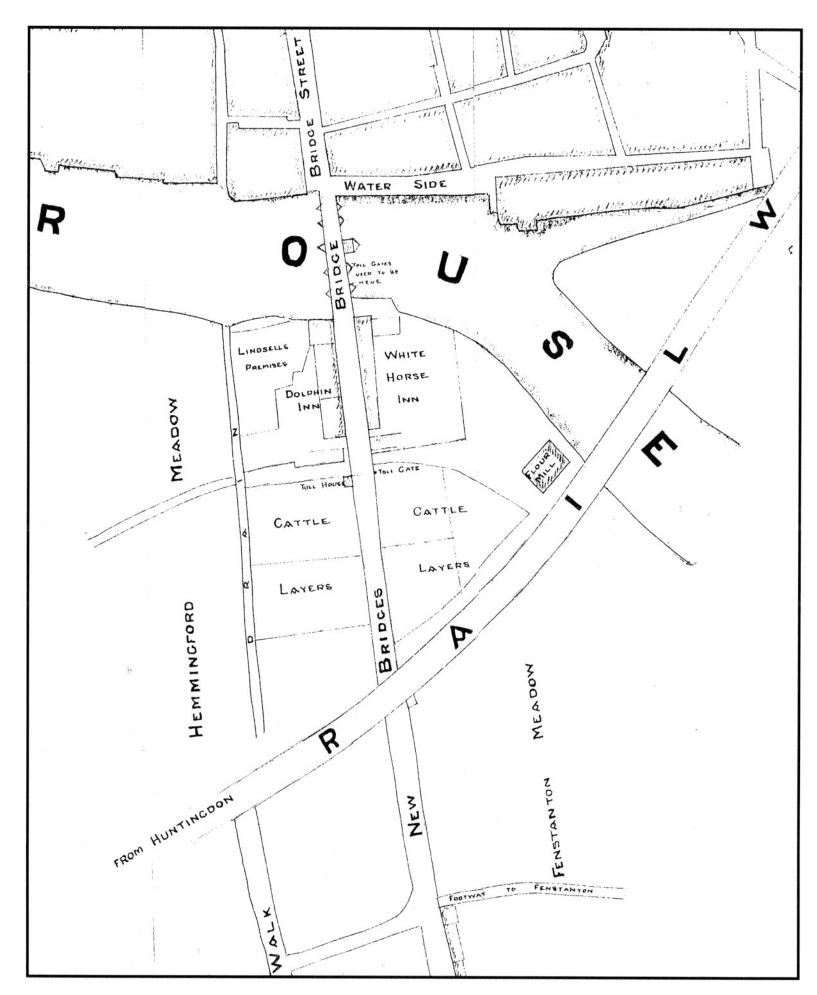

Fig.38 'Plan of the Town of St Ives' by Robert Hutchinson

Here is the important interchange of road, river and rail at St Ives in the mid 19th century. In 1854 Potto Brown had built the mill to the most modern design and sited it near the New Bridges where it could also benefit from railway and river transport facilities.

Robert Hutchinson was a local architect and surveyor. He designed the Priory and the Corn Exchange in St Ives, and the George Hotel in Huntingdon

County Record Office, Huntingdon MII, 73

Fig. 39 The toll booth on the New Bridges
The Duke of Manchester used the site of the New Bridges turnpike toll house to build a toll booth where his river tolls were to be collected; the site was convenient to the towpath along the Hemingford and Wilhorn Meadows. These 'Passage Tolls' were only due for the 40 days of Lent; they probably originated in the 12th and 13th century when they were collected from boats coming up-river with merchandise for the St Ives Fair held immediately after Easter. In the mid 19th century the use of the toll booth on St Ives Bridge was discontinued and the Duke's tolls – both river and Bridge - were collected on the New Bridges. The last collector of tolls was Mr Ted Gurry. When all toll collecting was abandoned after the County Council acquired St Ives Bridge and the New Bridges, the little brick toll booth with an improbably high chimney was used as a store by the town's road sweeper. The toll booth was not demolished until the 1980s.

Fig.40 A train from Godmanchester approaching the New Bridges crossing
The wooden trestle bridges carried the railway above the Hemingford Meadow and over the New Bridges. The combination of the level crossing on the New Bridges and the traffic lights at St Ives Bridge often caused long traffic jams, particularly if the train time coincided with the end of a shift at the Mill.
Photo courtesy of V. Webster

Fig. 41 Floods at the New Bridges in the late 19th century
A wide expanse of Wilhorn meadow is under water, but St Ives' road and rail transport are above the floods on the causeways of the New Bridges and the railway trestle bridges.
County Record Office, Huntingdon WH2/12

Fig. 42 Congestion in Bridge Street before the by-pass was built
A long queue of vehicles can be seen waiting at the traffic lights; queues often stretched back into Crown Street.
Norris Museum *PH/S.IVE/Bdge.St/20* *Photo courtesy of Civic Society, St Ives*

20th Century St Ives; another new bridge and causeway

The 20th century saw another revolution in transport – the development and rapid proliferation of the combustion engine. St Ives' streets and bridges had been built for horse-drawn vehicles and pedestrians, but became clogged with traffic when the old town was overwhelmed by cars and lorries. At its worst, in 1976, an average 11,000 vehicles per 16-hour day crossed the river on the 12' 6" wide medieval bridge. Everyone agreed that a by-pass was necessary for the town. Cambridgeshire County Council drew up plans in 1968 for a new road and river crossing to the west of the New Bridges and the St Ives Bridge. From the south, the by-pass road would divert westwards before the New Bridges, cross the Hemingford Meadow, bridge the river at Ingle Holt Island and then join with the Ramsey Road at its junction with The Waits.

A group of St Ivians were horrified to learn of this proposal and feared that it would cause irrevocable damage to the historic town - it must be remembered that there was no conservation area in St Ives until 1972, and also little protection for old buildings through today's 'Listing' process. A general meeting was called and 'The Civic Society of St Ives' was formed with 100 members and Mr Humphrey Warren elected as chairman. This new society was determined to fight to protect St Ives and began battle with the County Council. The campaign for an eastern route for the by-pass gained widespread support from local people, the Borough Council, the District Council and the Divisional Road Engineer, yet the County Council refused to countenance anything but a western route. In 1972 the Department of the Environment called for a Public Inquiry. The Civic Society was the principal objector to the County Council, and had to employ professional expertise to represent their case - counsel, solicitor and planning consultant. They had expected the Inquiry to last for two days and their available funds were overstretched when the hearing continued for seven days. To their credit, the Civic Society persevered, gave everything they had to the case, and won.

The spendid new by-pass and river bridge freed the town from its traffic problems. It was opened in 1980 having cost £2,500,000. Some years later it was named ‘Harrison Way’ in honour of Mr Bill Harrison, the secretary to the Civic Society, and his sister Miss Molly Harrison who had both worked passionately to achieve the eastern by-pass route for St Ives.

The opening of the by-pass brought a fundamental change to St Ives – it altered the main gateway to the town. The ancient route over the causeway and river bridge to St Ives was closed when ‘London Road’ became a dead-end, redundant for all but local access traffic. Bridge Street was changed from being one of the major arteries of the town into a side street.

Changes around the New Bridges

There have been many changes around the New Bridges since their construction. In 1854 Mr Potto Brown built a large steam-driven corn mill on the southern bank of the river to the east of the New Bridges, and a private siding from the new railway was brought into the mill. In 1902 the mill became a printing works, first to print the labels for Chivers’ jam-jars and later as Enderby’s general printing works. Sinclair Radionics moved into the mill in 1971, and here Sir Clive Sinclair produced the world’s first pocket calculator. In 1998 the mill was converted into flats and a development of town houses with a small marina was built alongside the New Bridges.

Fig. 43 Summer floods: June 15th 1954
This photo shows several 'landmarks' of St Ives that have since been demolished; the sheds and chimney at Enderby's Mill, the railway across the New Bridges, Bridge House and the old 'Dolphin' and, in the bottom right of the picture, the terrace of houses along Filberts' Walk, Hemingford Grey.
Photo courtesy of Simmons Aerofilms Ltd. A54711

Fig. 44 The opening of the by-pass, October 1980
Lt-Col. The Hon. Peter Brassey, Lord Lieutenant of Cambridgeshire performed the official opening ceremony of the new bridge and road on a cold, windswept morning.
Norris Museum, St Ives *PH/S.IVE/Aerial/1980*

Fig. 45 Harrison Way naming ceremony
l to r: Grenville Dodson, John Rignall, Pree Newbon, ?, Molly Harrison, Betty Harrison, Tim Harrison, Molly Bryant, Mark Plews, Hedley Grabaskey, Peggy Seamark, Jack Harrison.
Photo courtesy of Tim George

Fig. 46 The New Bridges and Enderby's Wharf
A new development of town houses with a small marina was built adjoining the mill in 1998. These houses are close to the northern, downstream side of the New Bridges; the raised level of the houses and their access road has resulted in severely restricted flood flows through at least one third of the arches of the New Bridges.

The 'White Horse' was requisitioned by the military during World War I, and after the war never re-opened as a hotel. Some parts of the building immediately next to St Ives Bridge remain and have been converted into apartments.

Across the road the 'Dolphin Hotel' functioned until 1968. After it closed to business its buildings became derelict and were demolished. Bridge House, next door to the 'Dolphin', suffered the same fate and was demolished in 1967 after being derelict for some years. A new 'Dolphin Hotel' opened in 1985 and incorporated the site where Bridge House had once stood. The land immediately to the south of the 'Dolphin' and next to the New Bridges became the car park for the hotel. In the 19th century and earlier this area had been used as 'cattle layers' – pasture where cattle were held while waiting to come to market. When the circus came to St Ives some of its animals were kept in the 'Dolphin' stables and yard, and there are entertaining newspaper reports of escaping elephants around the New Bridges.

The railway from St Ives to Godmanchester across the New Bridges was in existence for just over a hundred years. In 1939 13 daily trains each way used the line, but there was a rapid decline after the Second World War, until there were only three daily trains in 1953. The Kettering service stopped in June 1959; the Godmanchester station and the line to St Ives closed in June 1962 – preceding Dr Beeching's axe.

The New Bridges in 2005

The New Bridges have been by-passed, but that does not seem to be the end of their story. The Environment Agency is planning 'The Hemingfords and St Ives Flood Alleviation Scheme'. This entails the building of new flood defences and a pumping station in order to ensure that the villages and town are safe from the worst floods. Design studies and modelling are still being undertaken but it would appear that, after 183 years when the New Bridges' arches were built: *for the purpose of carrying off the waters in times of flood,* areas around the arches have accumulated deposits of river silt. It is now proposed to restore the capacity of about 30 of the southern-most arches by lowering the level of the meadows on either side.

Cambridgeshire County Council, as the body now responsible for the maintenance of the New Bridges, has announced the results of a study into their structural condition. The Council is considering a range of options in order to bring the causeway into line with modern traffic weight and safety requirements; these options include, comprehensive repair of the New Bridges, or demolition and replacement with a facsimile design, or demolition and replacement with a new design. All of these options are very expensive, with projected costs of £3,000,000 - £3,500,000. At present, the future of the New Bridges is uncertain.

Time has taken its toll on the appearance of the structure; on close examination, decay and piecemeal repairs make the arches look rather shabby. However when viewed from across the meadows, the long repetition of arches make a fine sight. There is a pleasing harmony in their scale and proportion, both in relation to the landscape and the adjacent buildings.

The structure is protected as a Grade II Listed building and is surrounded by the Conservation Area of St Ives. Until now there has been no appreciation of the New Bridges in relation to other causeways around the country. Now we feel some pride in knowing that the New Bridges with 55 arches is the oldest, longest brick viaduct in the country.

When the New Bridges were 'opened' in September 1822, the St Ives Trustees must have been very proud of their achievement. They had built a new causeway which made a dramatic entrance to St Ives. 19th century travellers, elevated on horse-back or in coaches, would have been able to admire the town from the modern road raised on arches - and if there were flood waters beneath the arches, this would have added to the impressiveness of the whole scene. Those men of St Ives would have felt even more proud of their achievement in a town where the controlling power was exemplified in the text chosen by the vicar of St Ives, Rev Cuthbert Baines, to his sermon on the occasion of the start of George III's golden jubilee year in 1809:

> *Fear thou the Lord and the King, and meddle not with them that are given to change.*
> *(Proverbs: 24 v21)*

The New Bridges are proof of the change that did come to St Ives. We can recognise the long struggle that was required to achieve change in St Ives in 1822, and we can be proud of the New Bridges as a symbol of that independent spirit.

Fig. 47 An example of the present state of brickwork of the New Bridges A report on the New Bridges for Cambridgeshire County Council by WS Atkins, February 2003, using the findings of a detailed condition survey undertaken in 1997, states: "The structure is generally in a severe state of dilapidation, due to a lack of structured maintenance and unsympathetic repairs. The brickwork has suffered extensively from the effects of frost damage and differential erosion due to the use of hard impermeable mortar." The report concludes: "The structure is approaching a critical condition".

Sources

[Abbreviations: ***VCH*** "The Victoria History of the Counties of England: Huntingdonshire", published in 3 volumes in 1926, 1932 and 1936. ***HRO*** the County Record Office, Huntingdon.]

Introduction

The VCH, vol II p 310 describes the New Bridges as being built by the Duke of Manchester. This 'fact' had probably originated from the "History of St Ives" by Herbert Norris (1889), who had misinterpreted information given in "The History, Gazetteer and Directory of the County of Huntingdon" by James Hatfield (1854). When historians have relied on the VCH, they have been unable to find out more about the New Bridges because they have been looking in the wrong place – the Manchester archives, instead of searching the Turnpike records.

Crossing the River Great Ouse at St Ives

"St Ives Bridge and Chapel", by Bob Burn-Murdoch (1st edition 1998) p 43 explains the origins of St Ives Bridge, but is tentative of acknowledging the 1107 date for a bridge, and discounts the 1259 inquest recorded in the Placita de Quo Warranto Rolls 43 Henry III; a better understanding of the southern approach to St Ives Bridge now confirms these documents as important in describing both the Bridge and Causeway. The VCH, vol II, Hemingford Grey, lists the causeway agreements, and in the "History of Godmanchester" by Robert Fox (1831), details given of the Court Rolls of 1276 explain how the mill owners blocked the river navigation to Huntingdon. The importance of St Ives Fair is found in "The Fairs of Medieval England, An Introductory Study" by Ellen Wedemeyer Moore (1985). "Medieval Bridges" by Martin Cook (1998) emphasises the importance of causeways: *they were of equal importance to the bridge they served and should receive the same consideration.* For an understanding of flood meadows I turned to "Lammas Meadows" by Anthea Brian, (1993).

The Road to St Ives Bridge

"The Turnpike Road System in England 1663-1840" by W. Albert (1972) was an invaluable source of reference for research into the Bury-Stratton Trust and its background. The original Act of Parliament for the Bury-Stratton Trust and the renewals are in the House of Lords Record Office. Huntingdon Quarter Sessions Records of 1810, held in the HRO, vividly describe the quarrel over maintenance of the old causeway. George Skeeles' notebook is transcribed in "Notes on the History of St Ives from 1796 -1930" by John Skeeles – an unpublished typescript held in the Norris Museum, UMS/S.IVE/153. The letter from Joseph Harris, which includes Mr Welstead's suggested increases in the Bridge tolls, is in the Norris Museum, UMS/KIMBN/139; its relevance was only recently appreciated in the course of the research about the New Bridges. Information about St Ives' livestock markets and the drovers came from, "A Tour Thro' the Whole Island of Great Britain" by Daniel Defoe, (ed. GDH Cole 1927), "The Drovers" by K.J. Bonser (1970), *Huntingdonshire Livestock Trade* 1600-1750 by Stephen Porter in "Records of Huntingdonshire" vol 2 no 2 (1982) and "The Marketing of Livestock in St Ives, Huntingdonshire and its surrounding Region 1830-1900" by Robert Flack, unpublished dissertation, Norris Museum.

Plans for Improvement

I looked in contemporary newspapers for a report of the opening of the New Bridges in 1822. "The Huntingdon, Bedford and Peterborough Gazette, & Independent Press" and "The Cambridge Chronicle" are held on microfilm in the Cambridgeshire Collection, Central Library, Lion Yard, Cambridge. When I found the report in "The Independent Press" it revealed that the Bury-Stratton Turnpike Trust – not the Duke of Manchester - had built the New Bridges. From that revelation, I worked through 25 years of the newspapers collecting all the Turnpike Trust's public notices - about meetings, toll prices, lettings of toll gates, invitations for building tenders etc. Each notice about a meeting briefly summarised the main item of agenda, and so I was able to form a picture of the Trust's activities. (If any Minute Books had survived, the task would have been infinitely easier!)

Bridges, Arches or other Works

When the Duke was considering his case against the Turnpike Trust in 1833, his solicitor compiled evidence about the building of the New Bridges. These notes contain some extracts copied from a Trust Minute Book which explain John Margetts' involvement; they are titled *Case for the Opinion of Counsel on behalf of His Grace the Duke of Manchester as to His Grace's Liability to keep up and repair certain arches erected by the Bury Stratton Turnpike in the year 1822* and are in the HRO, DDM 75/4. John Margetts and Sarah Gardner are described in the "Victoria County History of Cambridgeshire and the Isle of Ely" 1992 p 395-402. I am not absolutely sure that Elger was the architect of the New Bridges; the single mention of a name is in the extract copied from the Minute Book, and is very difficult to read. The name can only be agreed as 'El?er of Bedford'. After considerable research at Bedford Record Office, the archivist concludes that it is probably Thomas Gwyn Elger. The notes on Elger's family and biography are: Bedford County Record Office, CRT 190/13X.

Nottinghamshire County Council kindly sent me a copy of the "Reports of the late John Smeaton, FRS" (1837) vol I p 326-333; this is his full survey of the Newark arches. Robert Fox in his "History of Godmanchester" describes the history of the causeway to Huntingdon Bridge and its rebuilding by the Royston-Wansford Bridge Turnpike Trust. The "Bridges of Bedfordshire" by Angela Simco & Peter McKeague (1997) is a splendid piece of historical and technical research about all of Bedfordshire's bridges.

The building of 'The Great White Bridge'

I learned a huge amount about traditional methods of brick-making from Tony Minter at Bulmer Brick and Tile in Essex. Two other sources of information were: "A Rudimentary Treatise on the Manufacture of Bricks and Tiles, containing an Outline of the Principles of Brickmaking" by Edward Dobson (1850) and "Bricks to Build a House" by John Woodforde (1976). Information about building work and brick-making in St Ives by John Skeeles in "Notes on the History of St Ives from 1796-1930" can probably be relied on; generations of his family were builders in the town.

Letters to the Editor

"Cambridge Newspapers and Opinion, 1780-1850" by Michael Murphy (1977) explains the social and political backgrounds of the newspapers. The letters to "The Independent Press" were a rich vein of information, adding further details about the Trust, local politics and personalities. In "Hilton, Huntingdonshire" by Jack Dady (1992) Mr Hewett's struggles with his neighbours are wonderfully remembered.

Mr Hewett's Revenge

The Writ of Mandamus is in the Public Record Office, Kew; KB 29, 484 & 485.

St Ives and Politics and Money

The VCH provides a good summary of Huntingdonshire parliamentary election results and their context. Election Poll Books are in the Norris Museum; they name every freeholder, give details of their freehold, and record how each person voted. Samuel Wells' campaign, and his upsetting of the Tory stronghold at Huntingdon was considered sufficiently significant that his address to the Independent Freeholders of the County of Huntingdon was printed in "An Impartial Statement of all Proceedings connected with the Progress and Result of the Late Elections", for the Literary Gazette, London (1818) p 146-147, held in the Norris Museum. Lord John Russell's unsuccessful struggle to retain his Huntingdonshire seat in the 1826 election is well documented from the Whig viewpoint in "The Independent Press" and from the Tory view in "The Chronicle". The extent of the Tory effort to rid the County of the man who was to lead the Great Reform Act and later become Prime Minister is described in "British and Irish Elections 1784–1831" by Peter Jupp (1973); on p 59-60 he gives *A record of election expenses, Huntingdonshire* 1826 which is sourced from manuscripts DDM 21a/8 at the HRO and on p 38-39 *How to organise a proprietary interest, Huntingdonshire* 1826 from DDM 21B/8 at the HRO.

Thomas Telford visits St Ives and admires the New Bridges

Telford's extraordinary life and work are illustrated in "Thomas Telford" by LTC Rolt (1958). A transcript of the report by Telford on the river between St Ives and Earith is in the Order (Minutes) Book of the Commissioners for Navigation of the Great Ouse, Cambridge Record Office. The drawings, including the one signed by Telford, *Section from Earith Bridge to St Ives,* are in the Cambridge Record Office, R59/31/40/105.

Justification for the statement that the New Bridges are a unique causeway comes from research with English Heritage into causeways around the UK.

Ten years later

The progress of the Bury-Stratton Trust can be followed from the *Accounts Ledger, Bury-Stratton Turnpike Trust, 1826-c1860,* 1896/HCP/5 at the HRO. Unfortunately it is for the period after the New Bridges were built.

The VCH records the Huntingdonshire agricultural depressions and the 'Swing Riots'. Hemingford Grey's 'Poor Rate book' was recently found in a Saffron Walden antiques shop; it is to be deposited in the Huntingdon Record Office. A letter from the Solicitor General is with the papers about the Duke's evidence to counsel, as described earlier.

The coming of the Railway and the end of the Turnpike

Information about the St Ives railways comes from, "The Great Eastern Railway" by Cecil J Allen (1955) and "Branch Lines around Huntingdon" by Mitchell, Smith, Awdry & Mott (1991). Mr Odams' letter is in The Hunts Post, May 20th 1905, and the negotiations for the sale of the New Bridges and St Ives Bridge are reported in The Hunts Post during April, May and June 1921.

20th Century St Ives; another new bridge and causeway
The archives of the Civic Society reveal the by-pass campaign and the struggle to retain historic buildings in the town during the 1960s and 70s: "The Civic Society of St Ives, Ten Year Report" by W L Harrison (1978).
"Old Industries of St Ives Revisited" by Ken Ballard (2002) and "The Pubs of St Ives" by Bob Burn-Murdoch (2000) explain the changes around the New Bridges.

[A fully annotated, referenced text of this book is deposited in the Norris Museum, St Ives.]

Index

Pages and illustrations